BOCCONI
UNIVERSITY
PRESS

Francesca Moriani

BRAVESHIP

The Courage to Innovate: Embracing the Journey
to Distributed Leadership

Foreword by **Francesco Frugiuele**

Cover: Cristina Bernasconi, Milan
Layout: Corpo4 Team, Milan

Copyright © 2025 EGEA S.p.A.
Via Salasco, 5 – 20136 Milano
Tel. 02/5836.5751 – Fax 02/5836.5753
egea.edizioni@unibocconi.it – www.egeaeditore.it

First edition: October 2025

ISBN Domestic Edition: 979-12-80623-77-5
ISBN International Edition: 979-12-81627-67-3
ISBN Digital International Edition: 979-12-81627-68-0
ISBN: Epub Edition: 979-12-229-8114-7

Table of Contents

"The" Challenge

Foreword

by *Francesco Frugiuele*[*]

"They are really doing it."

This book is the story of the journey of a leader who—as a rarity in the small club of CEOs—is really doing what she said she would do. A journey that is paradigmatic of all organizations that wish to move into the future. Francesca tells us, in the direct and unfiltered voice that I now know so well, what drove her to dismantle the traditional business model piece by piece and replace it with something that few have yet had the courage to build. It is therefore the story of the connection between Francesca's constant need for personal transformation and the search for antifragility for her company.

The first time Francesca told me what she wanted to do at Var Group I thought: "This woman is crazy. There is no way she is aware of what she is getting into, yet she is determined to do it anyway." I was sure that the CEO of a company of that size did not really want to make happen what from experience I knew would happen by following her vision in a radical way.

In 2022, in Italy, we were a handful of professionals working in non-hierarchical organizations. At our first meeting with Francesca, we were asked to transform an already very large and fast-growing company into an "open" organization, i.e. a company where responsibility is distributed, information is transparent, and bureaucracy is absent. And to transform it all, immediately. "We have already been working on this for more than two years; now we need to speed up and make it really work, this distributed leadership!" she told me.

---

[*] Co-founder of Kopernicana.

There, on the horizon, Francesca saw a new, dynamic, open company, where people would be able to make decisions independently and coordinate among themselves without the need for bosses and rigid hierarchy; thus, a company capable of generating innovation and value exponentially higher than any traditional company. But I knew—as I told her—that to get there, on a path of "progress over perfection," she, above all, would be forced to walk on the precipice of the loss of control, with a class of managers that would somehow hinder this transition; with a centuries-old organizational culture that would try to protect itself; with a whole system of beliefs, habits, incentives and invisible structures designed to do exactly the opposite of what she intended to do. I expected that in the face of this barrage—as many other CEOs before and after her have told me—she would respond "let's think about it" or even "let's start with something small," as I had suggested. Instead, she said, "OK, got it. Let's start." I thought she would gradually realize that it was more difficult than she thought, and that she would slow down. Instead, with each difficulty she asked me to step up my energy, to put in even more effort. Several times I said to a colleague, "these guys are really serious about doing it."

Francesca speaks about self-management, distributed responsibility, platform organization and how to overcome command-and-control management; and she speaks about it from her own history and in her own language; a language that expresses a dynamic balance between the mad courage of those who throw themselves into the void and the rigorous logic of those who see the connection between things that are happening now and things that do not yet exist. But most of all, she speaks about people, real dynamics, obstacles, fear and trust. Because if there is one thing this journey teaches us, it is that it is never just about structures, methods, or processes. It is about us. About who we are, how we work together and what we are willing to put on the line to build something better.

As you read this book, you will realize that it is not a manual, it is not a theory, it is not a case study. It is a story. A story that has within it the weight of transformation, resistance, and radical experimentation. And like all stories of true transformation, it does not have a happy ending. Because it is not over. And if all goes as it should, it will never end.

Background

Gran Budapest Hotel, Viareggio

If this were a film, not a book, at this point the voice of a good narrator would start up, with the task of saying something interesting, captivating, colorful perhaps, to warm up the audience and begin to attract their attention. In the meantime, a nice long shot would pass across the screen, the kind that is great for framing big things or landscapes, and perhaps a simple freeze-frame, in an artfully created play of colors and filters, would make everything start coming to life. In that exact movement, the voice-over would start, and maybe it would say something like this...

Upon closer inspection, it resembles the Gran Budapest Hotel in Wes Anderson's film *Principe di Piemonte*. Or rather, it resembles it, but in a way all its own. Not in shape or color, but in that monumental grandeur, elegant and orderly, which was reserved for large hotel structures built in the architectural ambition of the mid-1920s, which made them not merely elements of the landscape, but the landscape itself. With the added bonus, with respect to the comparison with cinema, of a direct view of the two and a half kilometers of the Viareggio promenade, just a stone's throw from a sea, the one that washes Versilia, that when it wants to remains indefinitely low and sandy, once again inviting us to take a stroll.

But these are pages about neither the sea nor the art of walking, and even architecture has little to do with it. They might have something to do with Carnival, perhaps. But more than with Carnival in a strict sense, I would say that the real common trait is the one behind the popular anniversary at the beginning of the year: the awakening of vitality that becomes rebirth, in a motion of reversal that eventually balances things out again. All this is imbued and immersed in a kind of "culture of celebration," as a celebratory moment to be cut out from the ordinariness of routine, in which the veil of the ordinary is lowered and with it our guard is lowered as well, in a moment that is necessary, healthy and serves to recharge our batteries and be "reborn," and thus, finally, to be able to move forward. Provided that this partying, this celebrating, this having fun is recognized in the public square with dignity; that is, that it is institutionalized in some form...

Cut. This is as far as the hypothetical director-voiceover tandem would go. But this is not a film; the pages you have in your hands testify to that. A book is a book also because its frames must be constructed not with images, filters and slow motion, but word by word. And because the voiceover here, instead of speaking, has to write. Then, when the voice in question is my own, I prefer to move on, at least now that we have begun to break the ice, to things that are perhaps less poetic, but infinitely more in touch with my personal history. Which I would start, as far as we are concerned, exactly like this.

Kick Off

Var Group is not just a company, but an engine of transformation for the future of business. With a presence in 13 countries, it does not aspire to be "the best company *in* the world," but "the best company *for* the world," guiding organizations in their digital evolution with innovative and tailor-made solutions. At the heart of the Software and System Integration (SSI) of Sesa, the Italian leader in technological innovation, it develops advanced models that enhance digital excellence, accelerate competitiveness and open up new opportunities for growth, in Italy and worldwide.

At Var Group, the start of each new calendar year literally means: Kick Off. The classic event to begin the next twelve months, which every structured company carefully prepares and puts on the calendar to give itself a starting point; the moment from which all that is needed (objectives, strategies, etc.) can then be derived to bring the year to a successful close.

The Kick Off at the beginning of 2015 was my first; or, at least, in a way it was. It was my first one from within the Var Group, because officially speaking I had joined in the previous February, with Kick Off 2014 already in the past and by choice keeping myself off any stage. It was not really the first, though, because I had already participated in the previous editions, since I was regularly invited due to working as a distributor within the Group. So the Kick Off at the *Principe di Piemonte* hotel in Viareggio was far from an unknown event for me. It was a tradition that stuck with me above all because it was deeply rooted in an established order: an event that was limited in time, made up of work—a lot of work, all work—followed by a lunch that was the prelude to going home. There was little time for partying, just as little entertainment, and we invariably met up again the following year. Same place, same vibe.

I had never had to develop a critical reflection on the Kick Off itself; there was no need to do so, and it was not for me to judge or make comparisons with respect to my personal taste. However, the daily experience I had of work in the broad sense, and of my specific work at Computer Gross, suggested something to me. That something (which I would carry with me after 2015 as well) was this: work is done with colleagues, and to relate and work side by side you need a great deal of respect; to really respect each other, to find each other and get somewhere together, you first have to get to know each other, not in terms of positions but as people; and youth teaches that the best time to get to know each other is in a relaxed situation. Consequently, it was my conviction that, in order to work really well, it had to be done by resorting to an alchemy of factors, and these factors all had to be unlocked starting with moments in which people let their guard down, and quite simply, had fun together. Because only this way could people really get to know each other. Only this way could masks be set aside, allowing people to see each other (not just with fleeting glances), study each other, and accept each other for what they really were, and thus build something together.

January 22, 2015

Now this was my conviction, although not a very private one, that I strove to put into practice day after day. It was my own thing, at most it extended to the colleagues I worked with! It would remain so—a very personal distillation of life—at least until 2015. Because on my path that year was Viareggio, the *Principe di Piemonte*, the 22nd of January and a new edition of the Kick Off.

The ingredients for a good Kick Off are: choose a specific date, get a nice location, decorate it to your liking, draw up a detailed list of who you want to attend, inside and outside the company, and then invite, invite, invite. Also, draw up an agenda, decide who is going to speak and about exactly what, harmonize the order of speeches so that content and objectives "speak" to each other, and then structure the activities and their presentations. Finally, work on the collateral, i.e. everything that can be used to garnish the event: coffee breaks, lunches, dinners, possible inspirational moments or lunches, team building, and so on.

Carefully choose a watchword for your event, around which everything revolves, and which therefore acts as a leitmotif for everything that is said, shown, and experienced. Then let darkness fall in the room, while everyone is seated, and make the most of the size of the screen on which you will be projecting, the acoustics of the room, and your sound system. Play with effects, images, and sounds more than with "simple" text. Make sure that those in the audience have something to remember about their participation, something not only professional, but personal, intimate if possible. And, if you know and want to dare, put your signature on it in some way.

Much of this, with the necessary customizations to be put in place of course, I actually already had at my disposal; a consolidated tradition... A consolidated tradition around the eternal location of Viareggio's *Principe di Piemonte*. A set of operating procedures inherited over the years, duly tested and broken in, Kick Off after Kick Off. A team that continued to grow, in terms of numbers and expertise, starting from the historical nucleus of the equally historical Sesa, a company born in 1973 that had written dense and important pages of entrepreneurship in my and our territory, born from the dream of two enterprising young men (Piero Pelagotti and Paolo Castellacci), computer scientists at ISOR (a clothing company in the Empoli area that churned out aprons for first communions, hence the so-called "*isoretti*"), who one fine day in the midst of the austerity of the energy crisis thought of setting up a data processing center to respond to the needs of the clothing companies active in the area. In short, I already had a lot in hand, but something told me that "a lot" was not really "everything"—not for me, at least.

My first time

I started to organize that "first" Kick Off with the supervision and help of Giovanni Moriani—who had set foot in Sesa in 1978, as a programmer escaping from the fog of his previous job in the town of Suzzara. He was also very young and just as visionary, and the leader of Var Group at the time. Working side by side with the marketing team, the first thing I decided to change was the duration of the event: no longer just one day, but two. With the start of the proceedings in the afternoon of day 1, which was the more official part, an initial, introductory moment in which goals were set, stories were told, and everything that had been done in the previous year was reviewed. And a day 2 devoted to activities that were not narrative or celebratory, but operational. As a surprise, we arranged for anyone participating to stay overnight between the first and second days.

Now, the distance between Empoli—Var Group's headquarters—and Viareggio is not very long, and an hour's drive easily takes you from one to the other. What mattered to me, however, was to make others realize that participating in that two-day event was the equivalent of moving into a space "other" than the one experienced on a daily basis. To go to the Kick Off was to mean pulling the plug on routine in a certain sense, to step into an "elsewhere" totally separate from "normality." An "elsewhere" where one could (finally) think first and foremost about recharging one's batteries. And then there was the dinner. Which, incidentally, was still a "vintage" moment, in the sense that it required all participants to be seated, and thus still involved somewhat rigid and predefined positions. Now it is no longer fashionable to dine at a table (and today there are so many of us, with the trouble of finding enough tables...), and in any case the table in a certain way forces one to spend most of the time with the same people.

As a corollary, we had also hired a band, made up of a group of acquaintances who in addition to the usual tours of clubs and bars, had taken on this task of lightening the mood with music (which was to become a constant feature of our Kick Off, perhaps the only element that would remain completely unchanged over the next ten years). Thus far, the Kick Off as I had conceived it, organized it, and planned it "on paper." But if any of you, invitation in hand, had joined us at that two-day event, already looking into the *Principe di Piemonte* hall where the proceedings were held, you would have noticed something peculiar.

Something had changed

That something has perhaps already been hovering in the air based on what you have read so far, but at the start of the event it condensed and took a precise form. And the form was that of... a jar. Until 2015, and also due to a certain formal tendency that permeated many companies, including Var Group, working hours had a code whereby the seriousness of the work had to be reflected first of all in the clothing. Clothes made the person: this meant, literally, a suit and tie for the men. Giovanni Moriani also put his own spin on it, because he wore a suit and tie every day, by default. And so, partly through the influence of his charisma, partly through mental habit, formal dress was a sort of uniform for everyone. A vast sea of individuals in which one certainly found those who loved that kind of attire, but also those who—due to different degrees of restrained suffering—felt cramped, oppressed, anything but comfortable in that suit. Hence, the jar.

The jar was an hour of fresh air designed for the latter group of people, but in a broader sense—in my mind—it was an invitation to anyone. *Take a walk on the wild side*, as Lou Reed strummed in 1972: step off the track, once at least, dare, and see what the air is like. In that very jar, in 2015, those who felt uncomfortable with the tie could get rid of it, leave it in the jar, and come back for it later (or never?). Giving up along with the fabric, possibly, some of that formalism which, in my humble opinion, was not in itself an automatic indication of skill, ability, competence or determination in one's work. Laying a little bare, because what really mattered was never what hanged around your neck, but what was inside your head and heart.

Let me tell you something that you will find all over these pages: what I have achieved, I have never achieved alone. Certainly because it was never something that was solely for my benefit, but the fact is that I always found someone to support and back me up. The story itself that runs through this book is not mine alone; it is a group story, to which I have only lent my pen, my memory and my eyes as a direct witness.

Laying bare

If you had joined us at Kick Off 2015 by standing right in front of that still-empty jar, you could have witnessed the first tie falling; which, for the record, belonged to the *maître à penser*, Giovanni Moriani. There were many ties to fill that jar, in that January some years ago in Viareggio. There were so many because a new concept was beginning to take hold, one in which I believed and still believe so much: everyone can and must feel free to express themselves fully. Every small measure in this direction (of course, always with due consideration for the context in which one finds oneself) becomes something great, if only it can make someone feel better. Starting with clothing.

The jar was a great thing, but it was not the only one. After the first day was over, when the goals had been set, everything that needed to be said had been said, and everything that had previously been achieved had been retraced, going to dinner the scene emerged – a magnificent scene, in my opinion—of a more relaxed than usual throng of men and women (their white shirt collars fluttered freely, while their ties hung inertly from the pockets of their jackets) heading first for dinner, and then for the evening. Toasting, raising a glass and—why not?—dancing. In a word: celebrating. For the first time. Together. And never mind that at times the situation could seem a little amateurish: not too many people (three hundred, like the Spartans at Thermopylae, but with a much brighter future in front of them), a trolley of liquor for the toasts, strictly self-service, until the drinks ran out, which was all too quickly.

Yet, all that quasi-domestic do-it-yourself was something extremely rare, and valuable. Because it built a new pact between people who finally had no qualms about letting themselves go, doing it in front of others, and giving the word "together" a new meaning. Those first celebrations went on until late, we were eager to explore that unknown dimension, and we wanted to savor it as long as possible.

Day 2

So, eventually, day 2 arrived, the day when we perhaps got more into the heart of the work ahead of us and the Kick Off itself. On that day we moved from "theory" to practice, from programmatic commitments to operations, and I was in charge of the introduction. I've never been a machine; I don't have circuits popping out from under my skin or cables to plug into an outlet. And that day, although it came after an absolutely encouraging night, I was vibrating like a violin string. To get excited means to live in the moment, it means to feel the importance of what you are doing, it translates into an awareness that you are not passing there by chance, but with a task to perform and a contribution to make.

My first contribution was clear in my mind. It was the signature I mentioned above. As I stepped onto the stage, despite the lights, I could see the audience, the first rows occupied by the founding partners, the hubbub dying down as I approached the microphone, the composed postures of those preparing for a new day and to listen to the words that would inaugurate it. There is a moment that has something sacred about it when you begin to speak at a mass event. It is sacred because it marks the transition from the chatter of before to the silence of after; although it lasts an infinitesimal blink of an eye, it is palpable, as it marks the total change of climate in the room.

Of that watershed moment all I remember is the deep breath I managed to take. The one that charges your lungs, stretches your muscles and prepares you to let out your breath. Above all, I needed to charge my lungs. And so the first thing that ever came out of my mouth, in full and complete awareness and immediately after savoring that eternal moment, was not a word, but a shout. *"Our first goal is... to HAVE FUN!"*

Just like that, out of the blue. Because, two days, dinner, band and jar aside, what I wanted to introduce, to reiterate, to affirm, was something that I felt was really missing. A deficiency that I felt could make all the difference in the world.

Having fun

Give meaning and purpose to the concept of partying. Because, at the very moment when I had defined the goals for 2015 and from 2015 onwards, the first of them to be assigned an "official" character was, in my view, the sacrosanct duty to have fun. Not so much fun for its own sake, but because introducing this one variable into the work equation could make everything infinitely better. That "having fun" was something we would carry with us into the years to come (and in time elevate to the status of a real culture). But which, at that moment and in that context, despite the strange, new atmosphere that had already been in the air since day one, rained down on the first rows occupied by the founding partners, generating a palpable shiver, the kind that usually leads to a fainting spell.

Giovanni Moriani, Alessandro Fabbroni (the CEO of Sesa), Paolo Castellacci (one of the two young men from the 1973 Sesa group, as such our "real" founding partner): I had them just a few steps away. I could look them distinctly in the eyes, just as distinctly as I could see their agitation (a moustache quivering for one, the other with a hand going to the frame of his glasses, or yet another fixing the curl of his hair). During that shout and also afterwards, while I was rattling off the other targets, I could clearly X-ray them from the stage, while, traumatized by that verb seemingly pulled out of nowhere as an imperative, and which was so far from the groove of previous history (of the Kick Off and not only), at the same time the classic comic book cloud materialized above all their heads. A thought that contained the blunt question: "What is this woman saying?"

"This woman" was me, on that cold morning in Viareggio, distinctly damp but slightly cloudy, with the calendar marking January 23, 2015. Francesca Moriani, almost at the half-way mark of her first year as CEO of Var Group. But who exactly is Francesca Moriani? And why is Francesca Francesca?

Who is Francesca? And why is Francesca Francesca?

Not even if you're Eddy Merckx...

What I often hear from the people I work most closely with—yesterday and today—is that I am very natural, that I am not afraid to lay myself bare. I am not afraid in the sense that I have no qualms about showing and revealing what I am and what goes on in my head; weaknesses included. If one wanted to dwell on it, there could be a million explanations. In reality, perhaps it all simply answers Ockham's razor: this is how I am; I do not feel the need to hide in any way. Besides, hiding would be like running away and, as Stefano Accorsi says in the film *Radiofreccia*, "I don't think you'd run away from yourself even if you were Eddy Merckx." In talking about who I am and, above all, why I am me, I therefore think it is worth starting from the fact that, when I was a child, I was always much more attracted to things that are usually considered more masculine than feminine. In my own way, perhaps, I always avoided being stereotyped by the expectations traditionally reserved for a hypothetical "female being."

To look at it more closely, my whole family history, perhaps, is somewhat of a clash with stereotypes. My father—as you may have guessed, the Giovanni Moriani in the suit and tie I mentioned above—as a good young revolutionary high-schooler, had recycled the attic of his parents' house in his time, turning it into a kind of free port for his group of young protesters just like himself. Within those walls, where what was not immediately needed had previously been piled up, with patience and a lot of elbow grease he had assembled a series of soft lights, a cheap system for playing music and even, finding it who knows where, a mirror ball, of the kind that were all the rage in discos at the time. It was the middle of the 1970s, and the urbanized world had already been hit by the storm of '68 for some time, but in the countryside that wave had arrived more slowly, and much later. So even in the villages everyone was making their own revolution, however and whenever they could. My father's revolution included a tent placed in the middle of the attic, deliberately set up for those who wanted a minimum of intimacy to alternate with rebellion and parties. It was in that tent that I was conceived.

She saves herself, the princess

Mom and Dad were young, frighteningly young, struggling with higher education and work still to come. I therefore often spent my days at Grandma's house. But due to the absence of rigid age gaps, whereby everyone in the family was extremely young, my grandmother also worked, so I was in the direct care of my great-grandmother. Around that same house were two uncles and a cousin. I often spent my time with them, so it is not surprising that I grew up with a much stronger interest in things and initiatives that were considered masculine rather than feminine. The approach was not only practical, related to games and activities, but first of all mental: all the little girls thought of a series of fairy tales in which there were princesses who invariably went in search of their prince charming, and then just as inevitably went off to the glittering wedding that was the happy ending to the story.

I, for my part, felt in this order: an absolute aversion towards marriage itself; a deep-rooted intolerance of the classic white dress, lavish and overflowing with frills; a deep hatred towards the obligatory, one-way ending, in which the princess of the day was always and necessarily saved by the usual more or less passing prince. "She will save herself, the princess. Will she be granted at least that, or will she have to depend on others?" was my automatic thought. Unabashedly "anti-Barbie," having to choose, I definitely leaned towards the Meccano.

In the mid-1980s, my father started travelling up and down the United States for work. At a time when Amazon was a dream and international distribution chains were limited, for me it meant being exposed to a whole series of things that, if they had a big market in the States and were therefore at the mercy of the population, could not be found at all in Italy.

From each trip my father would return bringing me a little something. Often, these were technologies that were totally unknown to us (and, according to the dictates of the time, totally inadvisable for little girls), which I personally liked very much and which deeply impressed me. Two examples of the lot. The first: a game that consisted of building electrical circuits, connecting wires and making a light bulb go on or a bell ring, on which I spent entire days studying the connections—in broad strokes, since I was very small—to create an ever-changing effect. The second: an early version of the iPod, when I was already older, which I stared at in total astonishment because it had no equivalent on the Italian market of instruments for playing music, and therefore, I did not really understand what it was (with use, I changed my opinion, finding it to be crazy cool).

Technological illiteracy, maybe

From all this, one would expect, as far as I am concerned, an inordinate technological aptitude. But no, or at least not in the most traditional sense. In fact, I have never been in love with technology. Not in the sense of nurturing and cultivating a real passion in this direction. Rather, I would define myself as a technological illiterate, in total contrast to my father.

What I appreciated, however, was the fact that I had those technologies at my disposal, which was a blessing in general, but also an advantage as far as my experience was concerned: at the age of seven or eight, when my friends spent afternoons and sometimes even whole evenings tinkering with the ever-popular Commodore 64, I could use an IBM PC (!) and if I wanted to play Bird Mother or the more classic Pac-Man, for example, I was forced to write lines of code even just to enter.

Having that kind of equipment normally at my disposal, which was far from common at the time, and having to organize myself in order to make use of it, meant that over time technology lost some of its meaning for me, and instead gained great meaning in its application in everyday life. For this reason, the "standard" passion that I might have developed for technology as such (which for me—I repeat—was not extraordinary, but commonplace, routine, even taken for granted) ended up shifting to the applications, i.e. to what extent using technology helped to improve my everyday life (as a child) and thus my business (as an adult). My fixation is not on the object itself, but what can be done with it. It is, if you will, a functional passion.

A genuine fixation

There's something that has driven me relentlessly, an enthusiastic fixation that over time has shaped everything in and around me, including my approach to others. If I had to use a catchphrase, I could start by saying that I have always been "super passionate about people." But "super passionate about people" in itself means nothing. Unless you bring out the whole world behind it. Which means first of all revealing that I have always liked to get in touch with the new, with what I did not know, to get to know it.

Anyone who has been in any kind of company knows that once a group is established, it has its habits and roles etched in stone. In the presence of new people, it is almost automatic to be suspicious, to avoid them, even to glare at them. It happens to many, and it also responds to a certain biological norm according to which, in a group that has found its routine stability, any element "other" than the normal equilibrium can constitute a threat. Well, not only did I not perceive any threat, but I was the one who went to the newcomer and did the honors, talked to him to find out who he was, where he came from, what his interests were, etc. Both as a child and as an adult. Always in the same way, unchanged as the seasons, schools and ages varied. Perhaps this is a very practical and basic application of the infamous concept of inclusion that we talk so much about today. As it happens, this was my attitude from the very beginning. I cared that those around me felt good; that no one ended up feeling excluded in any form; and that everything ran as smoothly as possible for everyone. That meant striving to have an eye not only for "who" (so as not to exclude anyone), but also for "what." My concern was also to avoid wasting time in the usual dilemma—also common to any group—of choosing what to do.

Listen, don't give orders

This is also why, in the group, I did everything possible and impossible to contribute to things to be done that brought people together even when they were very different from each other. To achieve this, however, I had to make a lot of effort; to strive to listen, first of all; and to beware, as if it were the plague, of any temptation to impose or command. Because you can be born bossy, or become bossy. You can be that way always, often, or even only on certain occasions. A bossy attitude can also come from someone you do not expect, if they let their guard down just enough. It can be a matter of opportunity that, just as in the proverb, "temptation leads to crime." That is why I went, came, listened, reported and mediated. Years later—and after still more years of active practice – I would say that I recommend this effort at listening as a quick shock therapy for despotic temptations. There was no way I could avoid it, especially since the comings and goings were a perfect response to my quest to help make the whole group feel good. For such a project you can sacrifice yourself. You can accept fatigue. And you can even come to terms, in a certain way, with your own nature. Even I was able to do it, one who grew up exuberant and restless.

I am that way in part, and in part I became that way, thanks to that strange, wonderful family where we were all close in terms of age, we made quick progress, and you could mistake a mom and dad for an aunt and uncle, an uncle for a brother or great-grandmothers for grandmothers. Be that as it may, inside me there was so much rebellion. At home I was a beast at times: I did not respect the rules and I was constantly trying to assert a strong character, the kind you struggle to keep in check. The inevitable friction was with my father, who had the same strong character of his own. What ensued was a relationship of tension and conflict, which Dad had to deal with at home, and in the meantime he also had to keep his work-related nervousness at bay, since outside the home the company was growing from small to large, and as such was facing the market head-on, sometimes encountering moments that were anything but easy. But I was charging straight ahead.

Pian degli Ontani

Today, Pian degli Ontani (Alder's Plane) has less than four hundred souls who, as permanent residents of the village in the province of Pistoia, guard the Sestaione Valley out of season, in what was once a transit area for shepherds travelling with their herds. These few but good people, who talk about the places of their daily lives using nicknames like the ones they give each other (Diavolo, Peppe Padella, Sette e mezzo, etc.), are joined by vacationers when the summer season arrives, attracted by the chestnut forests and, as they climb in altitude, beech and fir trees, or by the wells and streams that shape the narrow relationship with the water of this small piece of land that is still Tuscany and not yet Emilia.

Pian degli Ontani is where, in the church of the Madonna del Selva Nera (today the Madonna di Montenero), the bells are still rung by force of people's arms, on the piazza dell'Acerone, a backdrop of mountains: Edgy, Craggy Peak, January and, almost next to the houses, the Orlando's Hat, on which Ariosto's Paladin is said to have lost his crest in pursuit of his Angelica. Narrow cobbled streets, ancient stone houses, and a secret village silence broken at times only by the lapping of fountains.

Pian degli Ontani—as I said, now four hundred souls but once five souls plus seven cats in all—was the place where I spent the winter and the theater where so many of my New Year's Eves were staged, at a time somewhere between being a child and becoming a teenager. On one of them, in my first year of middle school, for the first time ever, I was granted permission to go out to a party. At the age of eleven and in a world that still didn't know mobile phones, my reference for knowing when it was time to go home was my wristwatch. My father had taken me aside, to warn me that as an exception, since it was New Year's, I was to return home by half past midnight, so as to at least give me a chance to celebrate the New Year before heading home.

Too much nonchalance

Obviously, the intention was good and the conditions more than reasonable, this being my first evening out. Just as obviously, however, I had no intention of keeping to my return time. So, I merely moved the clock back, to create an alibi for the reprimand that would follow. At half past midnight, I did not return home. So my father, after having waited the necessary few minutes, came looking for me. Pian degli Ontani is neither Milan nor New York, and his search was resolved fairly quickly. He found me, and to his protests, with a certain nonchalance, I merely showed him the watch with the hands that at that moment (about one o'clock in the morning) clearly showed eleven twenty.

Perhaps I had not prepared myself enough, perhaps I had failed to feign surprise. Or maybe the solidity of the alibi was not as important to me as doing my own thing. The fact is that my father, instead of exploding at me or who knows what, looked at me calmly and admitted that he used such bizarre tricks before as well. So, now, head down and pedal home. Not coming back at the appointed time. Not coming back at all. Or, again, not doing what I should have done, what I was told to do, what was expected of me, what I had to do.

For eight years of my life, I was forced to play the piano. That meant attending piano lessons and studying sheet music for a whole hour a day, every single day. Hate, Trauma, Rejection. That's why sometimes when I had to go to a music lesson on my own after leaving the classroom, I would simply keep going and not show up. With the teacher mathematically picking up the phone and calling home to find out what had happened. With my parents getting angry and telling me that I had to go, that I had to do it because "it was the rule." Now, I knew that not showing up would automatically trigger the call, which would be followed by the usual diatribe, and that everything would end with the usual moral scolding ("You have to go, it's the rule"). But I didn't want to do that, and worse, I couldn't find a single serious and valid reason in the world why I should bow my head. So, I kept charging forward, and Mom and Dad kept tormenting me, and themselves.

The best and worst of both

My Dad and my Mom... I always enjoy saying that I got the best and worst from the two—then usually there are those who generously, or just with pity, encourage me by saying that I have taken the best. Assuming that I have something of the best, I have certainly physically taken the build and metabolism of my father, who as a good super sportsman does not put on weight even at a price, not even now that he is starting to get older. On the other hand, I did not inherit, and did not pass on to my children, fortunately, his decidedly pronounced nose. I owe my face to my mother, who is shorter and more prone to putting on pounds.

In terms of character, however, I am increasingly convinced that I have managed to take the worst from them. Giovanni is hot-tempered, aggressive, determined, a rebel who, just like me, had moments of revolution in his youth. In her own way, Mom is also tough and determined. And she is of strong fiber: she and my father have been involved in cycling for at least 20 years, and Mom often falls, breaks something (including her patience), and then gets back on the bike and starts again. She is someone who, if she wants something, pulls out an incredible strength of character from who knows where. If she wants something, even on her own and not giving a damn about anything, she gets there in the end. Without excuses, with firmness and determination. I only saw her fade away for a while, pulled by a certain inertia and with a certain degree of suffering inside, when we still lived together and she had to deal often, too often, with the friction between me and my father.

But it was just a brief moment, and to understand this you only have to widen the frame a little and look at what she has managed to do in life. When she was sixteen she was in the third year of high school in Fucecchio, she was with Giovanni, and, thanks to that tent that towered in the middle of the attic and a love that was great and freer than the times, she found herself pregnant with me. Giovanni found a job in Suzzara, and she packed her bags, with me as a newborn, to move there. In Suzzara, without the support of her family (which had remained in Fucecchio), she continued her studies despite having me, and persevered until she graduated high school (which, for the record, she achieved with a grade even higher than mine).

Rebellion, recklessness and ability

One might say, indulging in a cliché, that such tough cookies come from old-fashioned generations, consisting of people "made" of other stuff, with a different temperament and much more developed habits of sacrifice. People created from molds that are no longer used today. But no. Here, the stereotype does not hold—and if you have read this far, this should not surprise you at all—because the merit is absolutely individual: Mom is from 1960, Dad is only a few years older. They aren't "elder statesmen," they never were; rather, they were rebellious, reckless, capable and full of the will to persist. And then, above all, they were absolutely young. Again, no surprise: mine is a family of young people. Both Mom and Dad have siblings: two for Mom, a brother and a sister for Dad.

Little brothers and sisters, so much so that the age proximity between me and them is absolutely brief, an average of ten years and nothing more. This staggering, this imbalance means that my cousins are the age of my children, for example. And, above all, that I have developed a relationship with my aunts and uncles that is practically equal, as if we were cousins (something I could not do with my actual cousins, who were too young for me and therefore directly and inevitably became my children's "friends'). We are a strange family, perhaps, but certainly a close-knit one. And we understand each other perfectly, even between generations that in theory and on paper are different. And sometimes with absolutely preferential relationships, I might add.

In this exact sense, in creating a very special relationship with one of my uncles, my mother's brother, the common and absolutely shared passion for the mountains was a driving force. As a good, close-knit family, together with some of Mom's relatives, we had the happy tradition of going to the mountains together in the summer, so that many of us could give vent to our passion for mountaineering and enjoy climbing together. A large number of us, Grandpa Antonio, Uncle Giacomo, my dad and my mom, used to get lost in climbing; Grandma Lina and I stayed below and waited. And we camped together, some in trailers, some in tents, some (like myself plus my parents) in a *garnì* (the forerunner of B&Bs).

Uncle, brother, Giacomo

The setting for this August tradition, and for fifteen of my summers, was Pozza di Fassa, in the heart of the Ladin valley, 1,320 meters above sea level, which become 2,000 meters and more approaching either Buffaure or Monzoni. Today, a coveted destination for lovers of the Dolomites, who depending on the season, alternate between skiing and hiking trails, walks or thermal baths at the Aloch spring. For those of us with the mountains in our souls, it meant, in this order: the 2,500 meters of Cima Undici (Peak Eleven), the 2,400 and more of Cima Dodici (Peak Twelve), or if we wanted to go all the way, the 2,800 and more of the Torri del Vajolet (Vajolet's Towers).

At the time, the sport I practiced was competitive skiing (I will talk more about it later, for the role I attribute to it in making me what I am). Uncle Giacomo, for his part, was an absolute fan of ski mountaineering, a discipline that is more basic and older than traditional skiing, and which, unlike the latter, moves off-piste, involves an ascent with skis on and (originally) the use of seal skins which, once the destination has been reached and before the descent, are removed. This love of snow, moving over the white blanket, the ascent to the summit and then the descent to the valley, were the glue that had united us from the start. Add the few years that we spent together and we have the perfect picture for the fairytale of the missing brother. An ancient tale, though, and one that as such does not really have a happy ending—or at least, does not have one as traditionally intended. A bitter tale, perhaps. Because from the valley, as I watched him climb up the rope, anxiously waiting for my ten years to pass quickly so that I too could reach the right age to challenge the side of one of those familiar mountains with him, one thing I did not know, and could never have imagined: fate would never grant us the pleasure of climbing together, because that uncle so terribly close as to be an older brother would soon be snatched away from me.

He, who like me had that sacred fire inside him that blazes at the thought of the mountain. Molded by the same discipline that I felt inside and capable of pouring it into those ropes that kept me suspended until, having descended safely, tired and happy with the others, we were together again, sharing the taste of those heights where the sky seemed so close that I could put my hand inside of it.

The day of days becomes the hole of holes

I was twelve years old, Giacomo twenty-three. It was early in the morning of a special day, the kind that doesn't happen often, and I was lying in bed at home, calmly but constantly waiting for the alarm clock to go off. On that day, my undisputed idol was supposed to pick me up to go skiing together. I don't think there was even any light in the sky yet, but I waited, patiently, until it was time to get up and get ready. Only the alarm clock separated me from the "day of days." In reality, the sound that broke that fervidly precarious balance was another. The telephone. At that hour. Bad news on the way. Bad news, for which my family was not prepared, for which I could not be prepared.

Giacomo was very sick; the worst was expected and we had to run to him. A twenty-three year old boy struggling with death in his sleep, the phone rings, he's dying, run here. With something like that you can't come to terms. You can't. You have no time to think, only to act. At that point you run, you run towards Giacomo's house, you just run and try to get there as soon as possible. The distance was not too far, he in Fucecchio and us just outside the town, they are simple journeys, linear almost, but at that moment nothing counts. And when you arrive, sometimes it is already too late. Bursting into the house, too late, only to be told that the death had occurred. A big hole opened up in me. The day of days had become the hole of holes.

I was twelve years old. There are no instruction manuals for the drama into which I fell, together with my whole family, with all my being. No plugs to stem the tide that at the same time took away a model, an uncle, a brother. After that, for a long time, nothing was the same as before—and how could it have been? So much changed, immediately. Between crying that could not be concealed or limited, I was sent to the other grandmother, while everything was being organized, which just made things worse. Together we experienced the funeral, then I went to the mountains.

Starting to live again

My parents decided to get me at least a little bit away from that sudden, existential, total grief that had come upon us all at once. They sent me to the mountains with a small group from the ski club. And then, as I was skiing, I had races to take part in. Legend has it that, when something like this happens, one tends to respond in two very opposite ways. Either the race goes horribly, because one's mind is totally elsewhere; or, absurdly, the race goes very well because, in some strange way, in that tension one finds a moment of eternity, to re-establish a connection with someone who is no longer there. I don't follow stereotypes, let alone legends, so I can't remember anything about that post-Apocalypse race.

Similarly, I do not remember everything that happened in the days that followed. What I do know, however, is that for a certain period of time I stopped. I stopped doing everything: I didn't study, I went out, I was late, I didn't care about anything. I wasn't throwing a tantrum. Rather, I was coming to terms with a question that had begun to torment me almost fiercely. What is the point of studying, of making an effort, of caring about things and situations if it can all simply end like that? Now, the bitter ending would come right here. But under the ashes the embers can continue to smolder.

Perhaps Giacomo had not yet finished teaching me things.

From a certain point on, in a natural and almost automatic way, my attitude took an opposite turn. As if the stars had realigned themselves by magic, as if a stopped clock had started beating again. That black hole into which I had fallen made sense, but until then I had been unable to grasp it. I could not have done so until I reached the bottom. When I got there, I finally climbed again, and it was like being reborn.

Giacomo's last, great lesson for me was: life must be adored, there is no time for anything else, because every day must be celebrated as if it were the last. It is something I still carry with me, something that was with me when I signed up for my first climbing course, without my idol but with my heart and memory full of him, and when I started climbing regularly, for me and for him. Something I carry in my pocket every day, in the office as at home.

No excuses

Don't complain. Don't waste time. Always look for and find ways to achieve your own happiness, even at the cost of appearing a little selfish, i.e. thinking of the well-being of others but also of your own. Feeling good about yourself, with full respect for others. That is why I have an exaggerated aversion for those who insist on getting bogged down in situations that do not make them happy. For those who always look for an "if," a "but." For those who descend into victimhood. For me, these are people who insult life, which is one, sacred, and should be enjoyed. Day by day, day after day, because each day could be the last.

If everything can really end like that, tomorrow and in the blink of an eye, we have to hurry up and make sense of what we are doing. Put everything into it. Find that one shred of happiness, that one shred of serenity, whatever that means for each individual, according to their exact meaning. There is no one person who can tell you what will make you happy; it is your duty to find out. No one and nothing can condition you. There is no stereotype, relationship, dictate or rule that has the power to do this to you. If you live in a relationship that gives you nothing and you separate yourself, you have failed: wrong. If you are a woman, you have to do certain things, and submit to precise routines that punctuate your existence: nothing could be more false, forced or unfair. You must have the strength, determination and perseverance to resist. To learn to go your own way. To choose to do and pursue what gives us serenity and happiness, possibly every day. To stop complaining. To begin to perceive the good fortune that is inherent in our lives. Even if luck, per se, does not exist. Instead, what there is, and it must be deeply developed, is the ability to create the conditions to produce luck, recognize it and live it, whatever it means. Get things started, day after day, in the right direction. Ignoring the excuses, that are too many and too easy, available to us at all times, and that we could make at any time. No more victimization, no more excuses. Zero excuses.

How was Francesca the adult born?

Ten minutes at the most

Going slowly, but really slowly, with your foot on the accelerator and limiting the gas pedal to perhaps enjoy the scenery, it takes ten minutes at the most. Via del Piano, a mere 150 meters of Via Forestale, and then straight on along Via del Sestaione. In little more than two kilometers of road, curve after curve, hut after hut, tree after tree, we leave the tiny village of Pian degli Ontani behind us and, losing ourselves in those mountains that seem to be lined with moss for how green they are, we reach Pian di Novello.

The Sestaione Valley is an exact, high-resolution photograph of the Tuscan-Emilian Apennines. It is a corner of the world, carved out by streams flowing towards the sea and watched over by mountains and passes with strange names: Three Powers Alps, Old Woman's Pass, Old Woman's Tooth Mount, Elbow Mountain, Aviary Mount, Sentinel's Pass. In ten kilometers of valley, you reach an altitude of 1,300 meters; below 1,500 meters is a jubilation of beech trees that provide plenty of shade in the summer and spruce trees identical to those you would expect to find in Trentino. As we climb, the rules of the mountains change and the blanket of trees makes way for heather, blueberry bushes and rocks peeping out of the ground, the teeth of giants that have always been asleep. And then there are the fields and meadows, like those bordering both "my" Pian degli Ontani and Pian di Novello, which can be reached in those ten minutes or so, always going slowly, almost being carried by Provincial Road 20.

For those who really love the mountains, for those who feel it in their

blood—and from what you have read so far, my family is one that culti-
vates precisely this kind of fascination—for all of them, summer equals
the Dolomites, and so what if the journey is long, because the reward is
great. But winter, if you are born where I was born, if you have a family
like mine, and if looking at a mountain gives you goose bumps, if that
is the case, winter is something else again. If you have the slopes of the
Apennines just a handful of kilometers away, winter is Abetone. For me,
since time immemorial, winter was synonymous with Pian degli Ontani
and all the snow I could get under my boots at Pian di Novello.

Forward/backward, right/left, rotation, high/low

At the age of six, I did not know many things, nor could I even imagine
them. What I did know was that going up and down the Beatrice slope,
which at the time was the pride of Pian di Novello, gave me a great sense
of satisfaction. So up and down I skied the snow under the eyes of my
grandfather. Relentless as any little girl is when she does what she likes,
without stopping, without thinking about anything except getting down
and then back up. Forward/backward, right/left, rotation, high/low. I
didn't know many things, and that day I didn't even know that all that
activity was being closely watched not only by my grandfather, but also
by someone else.

Sonia Poccianti is at home in Pian di Novello, not only because her
family has invested heavily in the village, but also because she carries
within her a sacred fire, the passion for skiing, which saw her train, suffer, improve and persevere until she wore the jersey of the national ski
team. Then time passed and, like so many athletes who discover that
they can no longer compete directly, Sonia decided to work to help others
in the field compete.

As I traced and re-traced my trajectories in the snow, in that winter
when I was barely six years old, it occurred to her, who in the meantime
had become the owner of the local ski school and also ran the competitive
team, that I might have that certain extra, the right stuff. She watched,
watched again, and smiled. Then she walked a few meters, came up to
my grandfather and told him that in that non-stop, uninterrupted coming and going of mine, there was a method. That if she were him, she
would think of letting me try skiing at another level, that of competition.

Thus began, almost as a joke, my skiing adventure with the woman who would remain my coach for the next twenty years.

Today, Pian di Novello is different from what it was then. The lifts that had made it a great little ski destination have long since closed, and the undergrowth is forming on the glorious Beatrice slope, obstructing passage. On either side of the slope is the reign of the beech trees that soar skyward to the delight of those who now, guessing at the ancient paths and lost mule tracks, walk over that piece of the Apennines, ascending and descending without the thrill of skis on their feet, no longer in winter but in spring, summer and autumn. Everything has changed, but the lesson I carry inside remains the same, unchanged and unshakeable.

A ticket to competition

The invitation that came from Poccianti's intuition had become my ticket to competition, in a sport, skiing, that is a complete activity, in a sense that goes far beyond the healthiest meaning of the term.

Skiing, as I have experienced it, is complete because it is able to strip you of all your excuses and put you in a place and time where any excuse you might attempt in a team simply has no value. It is an all-round sport, because it strips you of everything and forces you to cultivate, assert and maintain an extreme concentration that is really all you have to take with you into "your" minute of the race. Because that's all the time you have, in a sport that occurs in heats of 60 to 90 seconds at the most, where your exact duty is to take all that you have learned, suffered, refined, and experienced into your own hands; drawing on your training, compressing and respecting it, and making it pay off by becoming worthy of the goal. Knowing, on the other hand, that you constantly struggle with imperfection, with that minimum amount of error that, while elsewhere it may count for relatively little, here makes all the difference in the world.

A dirty kick in football can still end up in the net, and the goal be achieved. An infinitesimal distraction on skis, on the other hand, ruins everything. Put like that, it would seem to be the absolute glorification of individual performance. But no, because skiing is also the sport of surprises. A sport in which the team counts as much as the individual. For me, as a "citizen," i.e. a child born and bred elsewhere, pursuing my passion for skiing meant dropping everything and leaving home for weeks at a time just to follow the team. Even if you are six or seven years old, you pack your bag for the team and with the team, get on the bus and off you go, towards the glaciers of Val Senales and Tignes, for summer training. And then you come back, spend some time with the family, pack your bag again, and off you go.

A world of relationships

There was all of this, in the vast sea of things you had to compress and squeeze into the minute of competition. And there was a world of relationships to build and maintain, in a team that was mixed to the nth degree: boys and girls together, but also boys and girls of all ages. People with whom you didn't just do sports, but with whom you lived and coexisted. People who earned a different kind of attention than that reserved for others, for the relationships you had and had to manage, in the mornings on the slopes and in the afternoons when you were not training, in the evenings at the table and at night when you went to sleep.

It was a different way of life, the result of a culture that was, of necessity, completely different from that of people who remained in their comfort zone, at home, surrounded by their usual more or less comfortable habits, and with more limited moments of social interaction.

I, and those like me who had chosen to embrace competition, had to cope with other people as best as possible, whoever they were. It was life without a filter, and it was not always easy (it could not and should not be). I often had to deal with real bullying, hazing or whatever you want to call it.

There was the "radio," for example, and I ended up locked in a cupboard and forced to sing, talk, explain or act depending on which channel the group decided I was to play. There were more or less atrocious pranks, such as sneaking into someone's room just before the time to return home, and knotting together (and mixing up) all the clothes that the four of us had carefully placed in the suitcases, not forgetting to also remove the light fuse, so as to further complicate the situation. All of this happened with a certain regularity, it was part of the daily routine, and the solution was not and could not be to go protest in tears. Rather, it meant learning to defend yourself, to live with the group in perfect autonomy, to survive in this world, because then the world is colorful, and you can and must know how to live with those you like as well as with those you cannot stand, and above all with yourself.

"Deal with it…"

It wouldn't even have helped to protest to those who were coaching us: they were people who counted on this autonomy and consequently invited us in various ways to learn the subtle but fundamental art of dealing with each other. At the beginning I didn't even know this, and when I first complained to them the answer was: "Deal with it, lock yourselves in a room, beat each other up, and then get it over with and clean up the blood."

At first it was a shock, then I realized what the "second channel" of communication was, the unspoken that was hidden between the lines and that made (and still makes) all the difference in the world to me. What sounded like simple blame-shifting was anything but: it was an appeal to the discipline inherent in avoiding getting tied up in foolish things, nipping them in the bud so as not to spend precious energy on them, and to cultivate a sense of inner autonomy that is the most solid prerequisite for living together. Competition or no competition, skiing or no skiing, away or at home, in sports as in life.

Control yourself and work on your skills, on being able to react to and face any little problem in order to keep your energy to spend on what really matters. This principle followed you beyond the trip: apart from team training, in my home routine I had a three-hour-a-day exercise plan, supervised by a private trainer who had received specific guidance from my competitive skiing coach, plus extra power and endurance activities to accompany it. You only follow such a plan if you are truly motivated, if you have the patience, stubbornness and tension to make it the pivot of your days. It is a real discipline, for which you have to be willing to sacrifice something. For years I followed it, day after day, with the rigor of someone who wants that one minute in which to go for it all. With the respect of someone who sees sports as something serious, something profound, to be honored, even when (and especially when) you normally don't feel like it, it's raining or snowing or windy or icy outside.

Competing taught me a lot, and this extra principle as well: if you decide to do something, accept the whole price of doing it right.

Every time I competed, and lost

At the age of eighteen, so many cards on the table inevitably get shuffled. It is difficult for a teenager to make a life for herself because she starts to have so many things on her mind. If you also carry with you baggage that begins to weigh you down, with all the agitated Saturdays and Sundays that you continue to spend training, and which necessarily uproot you from your environment and your friendships, from your free time and from what is impossible for you but almost flat normal for everyone else, then the going begins to get tough. Getting organized becomes difficult and it can happen that the wind starts pulling you somewhere else.

Competition for me started in 1983, the year the Internet was officially born and Snorkies and Care Bears were all the rage among girls my age, while the third episode of the *Star Wars* saga was released in US movie theaters: *The Return of the Jedi*. I cultivated that competition, undeterred, until 2002. It was almost twenty years of dedication and discipline, and I can say that it really taught me a lot, if not everything.

Above all, I had the privilege of learning something every time I raced and lost—to be honest, of the races I won, I don't remember a single one today. But the defeats, those have stayed with me, they are perfectly clear. One year, for example, I was in top form and my goal was *Pinocchio on skis*, the most prestigious junior ski event in Italy, which was born in 1982 and over time had become one of the five most important races in the world for people like me who were between eight and fifteen years old. Like all events of this type, it included a series of provincial finals, after which one competed for the regional final, and from there the national and international finals.

That year, the regional finals were held on the Amiata, while the higher levels were held on the Abetone. For me it was the perfect set-up, as it was the same slopes I used regularly. With great momentum I had passed the provincial finals and with just as much confidence I was approaching the regional finals, my mind already on the national championship that I would be competing for "at home." As always, it would be the best times that would go forward, and there were no surprises there either. I felt invincible, favored by the stars, and I had the feeling that I was walking exactly one meter above the ground. Therefore, I set off in a cocky manner, and arrived at the bottom with the same arrogance.

If

At the edge of the slope, as per tradition, the man I called Grandpa Antonio was there, Grandpa Moriani. My personal manager, who had made it his duty to accompany me to all the races, taking all the times and recording everything strictly by hand, as they used to do. When I arrived, the first face I looked for was always his, and in one quick glance I could read an interminable judgement on my performance. By blood or by passion, that was enough for us. I looked at him that time as well. I never expected to see his eyes open in amazement. A long shiver went down my spine, I got close and pulled out what was supposed to be a question and instead became an uncomfortable lump in my throat, exacerbated if possible by the exuberance I had brought with me on the way down, which increased and began to make my arms and legs heavy.

"What happened?" I swallowed visibly. "You didn't qualify," he said. Full stop. Freeze-frame. I shook my head: it wasn't possible, not today, not with that confidence behind me, and asked him to check again. He agreed, but the verdict remained the same. And then everything came crashing down. Above all, large tears fell from my eyes. Unexpected, uncontrollable crying, as clear as the disappointment I was experiencing, multiplied a hundredfold by the drunken confidence with which I had started. This went on for a brief moment, then I felt a sharp blow in my buttocks, and the trembling of crying stopped. Poccianti had come up behind me and, as a coach, had whacked me with a pole right on the backside, which had the same effect as a slap on the wrist given to someone in the throes of a hysterical attack.

Not because of the failure to qualify; the trenches are full of that stuff. She had done it for another reason, one that lay upstream and downstream of the result, and which was infinitely more important: because by crying like that, loudly and in public, I was spitting on all the hard, unrelenting work I had put in up to that point to face the race as a true athlete should. One who, win or lose, must strive, in the sun or wind, storm or clear, to stay focused. I didn't know it—and I would find out later—but Sonia was also giving me an ancient lesson, the same one Kipling had put down on paper in the early 1900s (in the poem *If*) to pass on to his son: victory and defeat are two impostors, and what really counts is always elsewhere.

Hunger for stories, and for people

One question would be perfectly legitimate: what is it that drives a six-year-old girl, apart from the permission granted by her family and the shared passion for the mountains, skiing, sports in the broadest sense—if you like—to put up with a routine that will bring her to leave, to go away, again and again, to accept forced cohabitation and continuous training? From personal experience, I can say that there was definitely a great deal of determination behind it, a desire to do something, and as mentioned, to do it well to the end. But I'm equally convinced that, apart from everything, perhaps the most genuine driving force was something else. Curiosity. Curiosity to know, to put a series of answers between me and the (many) things I did not know. Curiosity to see, to touch, to experience. To discover different things and to know the story behind each of them.

But to speak of stories is to speak of people: the facts of history are such because behind them there is always someone who thinks them up, first, and then works to realize them. So over time I have always carried with me a great hunger for people. A hunger that asks continuous questions. Why is a person like that? Why does he behave in a certain way? Why does he react in one way or another? At first I was not aware of it at all, but that hunger to know what was behind (and inside) an individual was a hunger to know his or her deeper reasons. Factors that called into question the way she had grown up, the life experiences she had had, the family she had been born into or had somehow built, and everything that had helped shape her into her present "form."

If you are born with this curiosity—or somehow you find it in you— and if your mother is a teacher with a deep passion for disabilities and who therefore studied to become a support teacher in elementary schools, the dimension of the other is bound to come into your grasp at some point in life. That point, in my life, came when I was in elementary school.

A long period of afternoons spent accompanying my mother on her visits to the boys and girls she looked after in the mornings as a support teacher. Thinking about it today, it is a snapshot of a school that was, in which teaching was more a mission than a job, and therefore knew no precise timetable, but rather followed the course of the heart.

Gut + brains

In the middle of the afternoon, in defiance of school hours (which ended at lunchtime), we would visit the children at their homes and spend the afternoon together, "simply" to let them know that my mother was at their side and that there were those who wanted and enjoyed spending time with them. It was in this way that I felt a sensitivity towards others germinate within me, between what I saw during the visits and in my mother's way of behaving. At one point, I thought that studying psychology might be right for me.

But if you have read the previous part of this book, you will know perfectly well that I am and always have been a deeply practical person. Dedicating myself to psychology, which required five years of study plus another three years to be certified as a practicing professional, and which was tantamount to packing up everything (once again!) and heading to Padua (Florence did not yet have a proper psychology department), with all the work of rearranging my personal and competitive balance, could not be a viable option. Thus, I decided that I would cultivate that hunger elsewhere, and that apart from the academic choice (which in the end fell on economics) it could find other channels to be expressed. Because "other" is not only and necessarily a person; other for me is also place, culture, and in a broader sense, everything that is not directly related to the usual. The new horizon, at this point, became a horizon of travel.

I had grown up becoming one of those people with a suitcase always packed under the bed. This was an advantage, in a way, but only in terms of method. However frequently I travelled, in reality the trips were always relatively short. So between training on glaciers and races, I had seen quite a bit of Italy, but nothing more. And then there was a thematic limit, so to speak: my and our travels, however varied, all stemmed inexorably from the same common thread, skiing. So I knew the Italy of slopes, glaciers and mountains inside out, but the rest, inside and outside of the national borders, I had to keep imagining.

From moving to travelling

It was, of course, a way of getting around, but it was not yet travelling. I didn't start travelling in the true sense of the word until much later, when for the vacation taken for my 22nd birthday, after summers upon summers devoted religiously to the Val di Fassa, my parents decided that they too wanted "something else." In fact, they had already started a bit earlier before involving me, and had discovered that their ideal trip was one where they could also do some sports. The sport was horse riding, and so in 1999, for my "baptism of fire," something was organized that was more similar to an 18th century Grand Tour than a simple trip. Five weeks in a row across the Atlantic, which turned into six because, not surprisingly, Giovanni had been invited to the Microsoft Convention, which was also attended by a certain Bill Gates.

Thus I encountered a world, not as new as the States, but very new to me. Day after day I discovered a way of travelling in which I had the good fortune to fully immerse myself in what I was seeing, savoring nature and taking in the sights of those who lived that reality on a daily basis. At the age of twenty-two, I experienced the horror of life on the Indian reservations through the nightly stories a native family told us around the campfire. I listened and asked and listened some more, and to fall asleep was very hard even when I was exhausted, because everything was stirring inside me, and not only because of the sometimes crude stories, but because I was taking a long bath of life at abysmal distances from what had been my ordinary dimension until then.

I immediately loved the journey conceived of and implemented in this way. I loved it and wanted to try it again, again and again. Adventure after adventure. I loved it so much that I cultivated it and made it a constant in my life. That is why, then as now, when I think about travelling I have to look long, far and deep, because I have learned that my curiosity has an immense and irrepressible range. When faced with a journey, a real journey I mean, I was and am always ready. And I was ready just two years after my baptism of fire, when the adventure was called Wyoming and for us it meant spending days of full immersion with a group of cowboys, taking part in such a titanic task as moving herds from one place to another, riding in formation during the day and opening our tents under a carpet of stars when the blue velvet of the night fell in the prairie.

After finishing there, with all the excitement of "cattle work" still on my skin, Vancouver awaited me with an unrelenting struggle... English. Because I carried a dream with me: a master's degree in the United States. But I also had serious problems with something for which I was not at all suited, the study of languages other than my own, which required an absolutely unpleasant effort: memorizing terms and vocabulary that I did not understand and did not absorb because they had nothing to do with my own experiences. Vancouver was not just a place; rather, it was a feeling and a last resort.

I had to learn English, no matter how difficult it seemed to me, and the only way to do that was to corner myself and stay there until the job was done. I was running out of time and didn't want to make any excuses. So, I left, leaving behind the one exam I had left and my thesis. Above all, I left, once again, forcing myself to return only when I had mastered the language.

Evidently, this drastic method ended up working because, at the end of the first month of my stay in Canada, the difficulty decreased and a certain degree of naturalness took over. I was adapting, I had adapted. The master's degree was finally approaching.

But September had also arrived, and the year was 2001. On September 11, I was in Vancouver. And I didn't notice anything at all, because at home there was no television and no newspaper, and just like every day I got out of bed, ate breakfast and went out. In the street, however, something was wrong; there was a general wailing that I couldn't explain to myself until I realized that everyone was doing the exact same thing. They were crying. Something was wrong. Something big was definitely wrong. The news of the attack on the Twin Towers caught me there, on the same continent but at an enormous distance. And that distance became something definitive. The States were no longer a desirable destination, and those exhaustively deep and totally unexpected wounds would take a lifetime to heal. With this in mind, and in the false expectation that something would somehow open up again, after two months of "watch and wait," I packed my bags again, for Italy. At home I found time. Not too much time, actually, but enough to draw up a list of universities that might suit me for a master's degree.

Brighton

My goal was to end up in an environment that had at least some of all that contamination my travels had exposed me to. Contamination of places but above all of stories, cultures and people. A multicultural university, in short. The choice fell on England and the University of Brighton in particular, which had the reputation of being a melting pot of peoples with the ability to build classrooms full of students from different countries. The perfect place to add a chapter to my life experiences. First, though, I had my last exam, and above all, a degree to obtain, and so I did, on June 20, 2002. Once I graduated, with registration for the master's course completed and a whole summer separating me from the resumption of my studies across the Channel in September, all that was left was Interrail, which I had planned together with Chiara, my inseparable university companion, to travel the length and breadth of Northern Europe, *Lonely Planet* in hand. But mine is a destiny that has always been in a hurry, and on this occasion it was no different. On June 25 I received a letter. It came straight from the United Kingdom; from my future university, to be exact. Which as politely as possible, in writing, confirmed to me that I was on the list for the new master's course. But also that, since my level of English was not yet up to their standards, I was kindly expected in Brighton for an intensive pre-sessional. The pre-sessional lasted three months, starting on July 1. My graduation celebration was officially over. And the Interrail trip with Chiara ended up in the same waste basket.

Campus is for kids...

Out of habit, as you can imagine, my suitcase was already packed under the bed. The time to take it out, book a flight, and off I went. Given the short notice (where "short" is an understatement), not having time to think about Brighton and its surroundings, I got a room on campus. It couldn't be so bad... Instead, I packed up again within a month. And I turned my back on the "damn" campus, which was putting me into a crazy depression because I felt caged, isolated and deprived of all those stimuli that could help me live the challenge of the master's degree with the right approach.

I found a house with a Spanish guy from Palma de Mallorca, a Brazilian later replaced by another Spaniard from Valencia, and an Iranian called Sel. During the day we would study and attend classes; in the evenings we would sit together and spend evenings upon evenings telling and retelling stories. We used to do this directly, when we were together, or we listened to the stories of those who knew one or the other and came to visit us. Each of those stories, even if we didn't realize it, presented us with a photograph of the world around us, of its old and new troubles, and how it all somehow ended up affecting our own lives.

Being Iranian like Sel, for example, was anything but easy in 2002. Because like it or not, one had to deal with post-9/11 outrage and a boundless tension that pointed the finger at that corner of the world. And as if that were not enough, this was added to everything that for generations the Iranian people, just like Sel, had to live through in their homeland, where partying was forbidden, where music had to be hidden inside car linings, and where the more daring built small distilleries in unlikely corners of the house to produce their own alcohol, which for those ruling the country was the devil. Being Sel meant knowing full well that it was forbidden for a Muslim to take a walk down the street in the company of a woman who was not a relative, that seeing girlfriends was something strictly secret, and not having the faintest idea what pork tasted like.

It also meant, on the other hand, that thousands of kilometers away from Tehran, in a more grey and dreary country, one could come across a university that didn't give a damn about borders, differences and nationalities, because it put everyone on the same level. And that in that microcosm, with the complicity of fate, one could, if one wished, carve out a free port in the form of a multiethnic house, shut everything else out and go back to being just one boy among a thousand. Taking liberties, speaking without restraint, especially when the beer is flowing, and unleashing the tongue.

"In that year..."

A multitude of individuals passed through our house. Armenians, Chinese, a Japanese girl who taught me the noble art of making sushi. Real and "exported" Indians, like my best friend who now lives in Toronto, where even in the home of ice hockey and maple syrup he still feels like a son of the land of the Rajas. Two Cypriots, one ethnic Greek and the other ethnic Turkish, with the more or less somber stories (of expropriations, settling of scores, barricades, vendettas, etc.) of that open sore in a small island that could be a paradise nestled in the Mediterranean and yet is not, while I didn't understand why I never heard the words: "I am a Cypriot."

There was a very dear Nigerian friend who had come out of her country for the first time ever and who I once stopped from eating the chicken bones at KFC, because she had been taught that you really mustn't throw any type of food away. She would have ended up choking, but instead she froze when I warned her, because while we were eating chicken with the utmost carelessness, she was a tightrope, terrified of doing something that would make her look bad in our eyes.

It was a monstrously large group, with such a wealth of stories and experiences to fill our nights between one drink and another. It was the closest thing we had to a family that year. I am a rebel, but I am also a child of rebellion. When I go back in my mind to Brighton and our multiethnic home, I think "in that year there was an intense visitation of energy," as Jim Morrison wrote in one of his poems. Our intense visitation of energy was not just a makeshift attitude, but our way of making and remaking the world, telling night after night, binge after binge, the stories of a strange epic, which enriched us by forcing us, in that exact year of extraordinary energy, to think, measure, compare and grow.

How was Francesca the manager born?

People

Today it is perhaps the most popular trend. One of the hottest fads of the moment. Talking about people, thinking about people, making things people-friendly. And then down with a whole host of gurus, more or less, who tell you day after day after day that in their work, in their projects, in their organizations (companies, parties, and so on and so forth) "the person is at the center," "people should be put (or put back) at the center," etc. Which of them, however genuine the enthusiasm, realizes that the issue that ends up growing around the person also involves something else? And that the something else concerns not the individual person, but what comes before zooming in on the individual?

Because everyone has their own characteristics, their own talents, their own way of thinking, acting and reacting. And they can give free rein to all this, or try to restrain themselves in various ways depending on the circumstances, the occasion, the moment. Everyone is made in his or her own way, and by making an effort to get to know the other person in depth, one may eventually come to anticipate his or her moves, to foresee them. But everything changes radically if the person is no longer one. If we are dealing with a group, with a crowd, with people. With people, the "rules" that apply to the individual no longer suffice. People are a different matter, they have their own mechanisms, their own balances, and they require a different approach.

In the eighth grade, in the summer of my sixteenth year, I had a great "pedigree" when it came to dealing with individuals. I had always been the one who went to a lot of trouble, going out of my way to involve everyone, to get to know the newcomer, to ask questions of those who represented something new from the usual. From the inclusive games of childhood to having to deal with so many individuals so different from me on frequent ski trips. From the afternoons spent keeping company with my mother's students to the countless questions that swirled in my head that would bring me closer to psychology. I knew a little something about dealing with the "other," with a person, we could say.

Castelfranco-Santa Croce-Fucecchio

Little, very little indeed, did I know about the "people." I would see, touch and learn, as always happens to me, in the most immersive way possible, in the first remnants of a June in which, after an incredibly good school year, once I had finished studying and with summer ahead of me, the need arose to cover the cost of a vacation. Which literally meant: finding a little job that would put me in a position not to burn up all the months to come by spending them at home. I was not yet aware of this but, pay aside, this would be an experience from which I would end up learning so much.

Part of my father's family had a solid tradition in the linen trade which, between permanent shops and stands, covered a market stretching along an ideal, intangible line from Livorno, passing through Castelfranco and Santa Croce, to my home in Fucecchio. On those barely seventy kilometers, scattered between three provinces, which from the Tyrrhenian Sea at Livorno cut through the area of Pisa to the gates of Florence, and which could be covered by car in little more than an hour, that part of my family had built up a small, diligent sales network in which there was room for both the permanent activity of the city shops and the itinerant activity linked to the weekly village markets. My summer vacation depended on those three weekly markets: Monday in Castelfranco, Wednesday at home in Fucecchio and Saturday in Santa Croce.

It depended on those markets, and even more so on the exceptional skills of my cousin Sergio (formally my father's cousin but, given the proximity in terms of age I have already mentioned, actually more my cousin than his), whom I would assist in the noble art of dealing with "people."

Working three days a week was not too much. In permanent markets (i.e. non-weekly markets) the booths work six days a week, but one had to get used to a whole series of routines. There were the "before" routines: waking up at dawn, meeting at five o'clock in the morning, setting up the structure first and then the goods, arranging price signs and various posters, opening the till, etc. Once that was done properly, in an orderly and speedy manner, and Sergio's wife had arrived in the meantime, the most important part, the "during," began. This phase took up most of the morning, until 1 p.m., which marked the beginning of "after," i.e. in this order: the departure of my cousin's wife, the sorting and arranging of all the goods (which had to be stored in good order), the physical closing of the counter and the return home, generally between 3 and 4 p.m., apart from any potential mishaps.

This is how I started out...

At the age of sixteen one can afford a certain amount of naivety, and I was no different at the time. So, on my first day at work, I was confronted by a lady who came up to me with determination and asked me quite naturally to show her some thongs. Stop. Freeze-frame like in the TV show *Ramsay's Best Restaurant*, with the color filter changing to black and white, and all the people in an infinite radius standing still, petrified in whatever action they were performing in that momentous instant. Freeze-frame, but no commentary by Chef Ramsay. Sixteen year old me had no idea what the heck a thong was, and in my dismay at the immediate sense that I was starting that day (and that job!) off on the wrong foot, I stopped the bleeding by turning towards my colleagues in search of the classic hint from a friend, which promptly arrived and got me out of trouble.

Then I started to learn and continued learning until the very last day. Today, when I happen to think back to those days, to go back in my mind to that continuous coming and going of people, which had its own particular tides and obeyed its own rules, for the sake of brevity I always take care of everything with a sentence (the same one I generally use to answer those who ask me: "But how did you get started?"): "I began by selling underwear." Full stop. Just like that, simply and to pay for my holidays. And, incidentally, I learned a lot of things that way.

I owe many of them to a living example. My cousin was phenomenal in his work. Because he was capable of "entertaining the crowd." Which does not just mean standing at the counter and waiting for someone to ask for something. Rather, it means knowing how to listen to what can be heard. Knowing how to see what cannot be heard, or what is perhaps not meant to be heard. Knowing how to remember all that is needed. And having developed great timing: knowing how to find the right word at the right time. My cousin Sergio had listened, seen and remembered the small and large details that, from the vast sea of people who crowded the market without interruption and without order, distilled and brought out the specificities of individual people. And he knew how to ask one lady if the dog had made a mess again, the other if the cat had escaped from the garden again, to ask one fellow if his uncle still had back pain, and the other what he had given his niece for her birthday two days earlier. My cousin was not a secret agent. Nor was he a fortune-teller. He simply had the uncanny ability not to let what he was told slip away when a customer passed by and struck up a conversation. Perhaps he was more like a sponge. He listened, absorbed, shouted and spoke. This way, he became a living, breathing piece of a market made of things (goods, counters, signs, etc.), and people were bound to realize that he was there, and want to interact with him.

Market lessons

Add to this the fact that he also had a certain propensity at times to follow "his gut," to be a bit of a barker and a bit of a jester, and we have the identikit of a customer-oriented salesman, who carries an aura similar to that which you would attribute to a good barman. That of the confessor, a kind of friend who, even before offering you something, wants to know how you are doing, and to exchange a piece of life and the road with you.

That seasonal experience, brief in its timing but intense in its manner, left such a mark on me that, years later and at the time of completing my application for my master's degree, I deliberately included it alongside my other work experiences. I did this on purpose and without any qualms, because apart from everything I have mentioned so far, which had been part of my everyday life at the beginning of the summer between the ages of 16 and 17, I saw at least two other important aspects in it.

The first one: my cousin had passed on to me what others, with many more titles than his and much more time spent among books, would have called "the basics of a sales profile": how to sell, how to listen, how and what allows you to understand that there is room to increase the margin, how to upsell. And then how to understand who you are dealing with, how to say the right thing to the person in front of you, how to do a proper analysis of your customer base.

The second (that was perhaps even more important): working, toiling together with my cousin, shuttling from one market to another depending on the day, starting when it was still dark and ending up in the blazing sun, taught me that every job is useful (but this is nothing new, and perhaps even sounds a little melancholic and obvious as a consideration), but above all that every job has a chance of becoming something noble. Noble if it is treated with the proper respect, if it is experienced without just doing the bare minimum, if it is thought out, realized and crafted not on the product, but on the person who will buy it and solve a need with it; but above all the unique and unmistakable touch of the person proposing it.

A job, any job, can become noble if it is treated as something noble. I consider this, and all the others, my personal "lessons from the market."

Connecting the dots

With the wages accumulated during that summer and the following summer, I was able to pay for my vacation. Then, having graduated high school, realizing that I would not become a psychologist and opting "analytically" for economics, I looked for other jobs to live on during my studies. In the meantime, I was experiencing the last remnants of a competitive skiing career that was beginning to take something away from me, not so much in the balance of my remaining free time, but because of a series of back pains which, more and more often, literally made me see stars. At a certain point, I realized that this pain had to be counteracted in some form. So it was that I first set foot in Studio Paulus, run by Paolo Bartolozzi (he and his wife Cristina knew my parents very well), who specialized in back problems like mine.

I started attending classes at the university, then went to the studio for postural gymnastics sessions, which were slowly restoring a modicum of serenity in my life. After the first three months, due to the fact that academic attendance was not compulsory, that I did not have much fun in class and that my personal coffers were definitely suffering, I decided to take the plunge and connect the dots. I would study without attending class, and in the time left free by not having to follow the class schedule, I would get a job to earn some money. As fate would have it, Paolo was looking for help in the meantime, because the gym was growing rapidly and he could no longer keep up with everything. The studio was a pleasant environment, both as a client and as a sportswoman, so I offered to go and help him.

The "secretary"

My role in the studio was... any role other than that of Paolo himself! A handyman role, let's say, being occasionally referred to as a "secretary" in front of the public, but actually doing everything that needed to be done. It may seem like a confusing approach, and perhaps at first it was, because in a growing gymnasium there are no pre-packaged recipes for what new things can come up and what is needed to make the machine run smoothly. Sometimes you don't even know exactly what is happening and how the routines that have been running the business up to that point will change as a result. But in that initial chaos, method suddenly took over. And that method has stood the test of time and worked for all the years—many—that I remained at the studio.

By far the most remarkable thing about working at Studio Paulus was that, in keeping up with the evolution of the business and the many new things that were constantly emerging, I had carte blanche. Which meant doing everything, but doing it—or rather, redoing it—my way. Buying a PC that wasn't there before. Carving out a small space in which to set up the workstation, apart from the reception desk where everyone presented themselves, and positioned with my back to the entrance so as to have a view of the whole floor. Creating cards for the clients, starting with the first one, which was for the initial evaluation; and summarizing the notes that I myself took, following Paolo as he evaluated the clients, a process which arose when I realized that the questions he asked each client were always the same and that some of the exercises he proposed were standard. And then I would set up another series of cards with formulas to open a subscription channel, which didn't exist at all before, with a series of packages and discounts included. I created documents, put logos everywhere, and everything seemed more serious, less improvised, as the studio continued to grow.

The more it grew, the more the revenue increased, and I managed that too, in addition to the payments to the team that made up the gym staff, which in the meantime had expanded. Some people would find such a commitment exhausting, especially if it had to be combined with studying. I loved it: for my age, I felt very important to manage that swarm of responsibilities. And then there was the wonder of trying to invent what hadn't yet been thought of, or even just to make concrete what previously wasn't even necessary to imagine. Not that it was always a question of who knows what kind of disruptive evolution; it was often a mere exercise in common sense, seasoned with the great satisfaction of being the first to translate it into objective reality and then observing its usefulness, both for the studio and for anyone who came there.

Grown-up games

As a good sportswoman, I could not fail to organize the studio's skiing week, during which we took the entire clientele skiing, families included. Skiing was my thing—there was no doubt about that— but the real fun lay in all that meticulous and patient support and assistance, in which I became a child again and organized "games" for people of all ages. Games which this time, though, involved travel, overnight stays, meals, activities, etc. Similarly, I used to organize conferences with the Duchenne Institute in Florence, a major partner of the studio and standard-bearer of postural gymnastics. And then the summer dinners at the end of the year. Here, too, I was dealing with a gigantic and complex game in which I once again had fun finding the best location, inviting speakers, searching for the most suitable restaurant and circulating the invitation as widely as possible.

Those were wonderful years, perhaps because I lived them quickly, but with the knowledge that I made the most of everything, knowing that each challenge brought with it an experience.

Studio Paulus has continued to grow; it has moved out of its location below the staircase in my day, with just three rooms in which we used to do everything, and has taken up residence in a beautiful gymnasium. I haven't gone back, but my partner did, a little more than a year ago. And he told me that, *mutatis mutandis*, the cards created twenty years ago are still being used there, with those packages of lessons and those series of subscription options, which in a certain sense are also my own children, and which continue to recite that: "if you buy ten lessons, it costs you so much; if you buy twenty, it costs you a little less per lesson; if you buy forty, fifty etc., the discount goes up further, and it all becomes cheaper." For me, everything was absolutely fun and wonderful.

Very International Management

Having replenished my coffers, sorted out the database, organized my events and helped get the studio ready for its evolution, with the prospect of Vancouver bursting into my life and the unresolved accounts with English to be settled once and for all, I said goodbye to Paolo and crossed the ocean. In November, with my pockets empty again and having returned home, the urgency of finding a new job began to be felt. At that point, I went to my father and asked him if, in the time between now and the new start I had set for myself once I had graduated, a hand might be needed at Sesa.

So I started a part-time job in the mornings, in administration and with a job that was absolutely ideal for that exact moment in my life, because it contributed to my finances, which were still shaken by my long stay in Canada, but left me half a day free to prepare the last exam of the course and to start everything related to the thesis I was going to discuss. On June 20 of the following year, I put the word "end" to my academic career, while still working at Sesa in the mornings. At that point, the postgraduate period began. With an imperative that, needless to say, was to leave again, and since the doors to the States were sealed due to 9/11, I embarked on that season of intense energy in the meltin' pot of Brighton where I would study International Management.

The immediate future of the master's program included a semester to be spent outside of England and also far from one's home country. So the hunt for a destination began, and a popular uprising ensued when we discovered that the list included a place like Tampa. The prospect became: six extra months of master's in Tampa. With a host of preferences due not so much to the fact that the university was solid, but to the dream of spending half a year in Florida. The temptation was immense, and on my side I also had a very close relationship developed with some people and cemented by spending endless amounts of time together. However, the investment I had made to forage for Brighton had been considerable (the master's degree had been paid for by Sesa) and to force myself further by pressing for Florida would have been very out of line. I could never have lived with that strain and I would have ruined every single day of that fabulous semester. It cost me infinitely, but I opted for the alternative provided by the master's program: an internship experience in a company. Here as well, there was a list of organizations to which an application was to be submitted. As a good technological illiterate, I obviously chose IBM.

At the time, IBM had an amazing headquarters in Paris. Paris did not cost as much as Tampa. I could work in Paris without getting lost in pseudo-Caribbean temptations. So I applied for Paris, which didn't answer. Paris didn't answer, but IBM did; from Dublin. Quite different from Paris! Not to mention Florida... And quite a bit more rain, even though it was late June. I had less than a week to find accommodations in Ireland. All I had left to do was to pack up, like everyone else who had lived in that extraordinary multiethnic house, drawing new life from it, and who now had to abandon it to move on.

I flew to Dublin accompanied by a providential friend who offered to leave with me without any luggage so some of my bags would be assigned to him. He helped me find a house (this time I would be living with a French guy and an Irish girl); he waited until I was settled in and then went back to where he had come from, this time in possession of his things, but to leave for Tampa, the destination that a wave of honesty and realism had blown out of my hands. I said goodbye to him with the same lump in my throat with which I had said goodbye to the others, that lump that assails you when you are aware that you are not only saying goodbye to the person but also to the whole piece of road we had travelled together. And I hurriedly prepared myself, in the little time that I had at my disposal—as always—in a life on the clock like mine, to start a new chapter.

Dublin

There are girls who live very well in their comfort zone: same friends, same bar, regular dates; an unchanging calendar of things to do, places to go, and routines to follow. It's normal, you may like it or not. I didn't like it. Not because I despised it, I just felt restricted, limited, because I knew I needed something else to feel good.

I had fallen in love with traveling, not for tourism but because it was a way for me to connect with new stories, lives, and people. I had made a conscious decision to continue my studies far from Fucecchio and Italy, and I had always chosen or found paths that would guarantee me the greatest possible exposure to "other" influences. Italy's skiing locales, Sussex and London; the Grand Canyon and Monument Valley; Wyoming, Vancouver, Brighton; Tampa rejected at the last minute, Paris considered but never attained, and Dublin on the clock.

Six months after arriving in Ireland, I had my job at IBM, a rock-solid determination to stay, clutched tightly in my hands, and the dream of a "multinational" career. I worked hard, kept my head down, and pushed forward. In a corporate environment organized into national teams (by country: France, Spain, etc.) and international teams (mixed composition), with team leaders, first line and second line, I made my strong ambition to be constantly challenged felt and valued within the Italian software group, interview after interview.

Interview after interview, I had spoken with the first line of software, hardware and services. I had collected offers from all the groups. But my goal was once again elsewhere.

Impossible

Break through and go straight for the role of Team Leader. Something that, if you mentioned it, dropped it into conversation, or even whispered it, always ended up with the same, identical response: impossible. Because history taught us that no one had ever started working there, in Dublin, for the first time, as a Team Leader at IBM. I like doors slammed in my face, prohibitions and setbacks, whether real or imagined. Because they challenge you, force you to think, and provoke action. So I listened to the string of opinions that seemed more or less inevitable, I listened to the end about why and how mine was a crazy undertaking, and then I went straight ahead.

I persisted and worked hard. I was almost there, I had it, I was flying high and equally sure that I would succeed in the end. With my weapons and nerves at the ready, I knew I would achieve the impossible. Everything was going as it should, everything was moving forward—and even if it hadn't worked out, I would have found not one, but a hundred or a thousand ways to get back on track, to go exactly where I wanted to go. Everything looked promising, but I had forgotten one fundamental thing: life, as well as ambition, discipline, determination, and hard work, is sometimes made up of unexpected events; and unexpected events play like Chef Gordon Ramsay's final scores from the cooking show, which can confirm or overturn the result. The unexpected finally arrived on an (as usual) rainy afternoon in late November in Dublin, six months after I joined IBM.

Just for a change, I was working. And I continued, at least until the phone started ringing insistently. Someone was looking for me, and judging by the number, the call was coming from Italy. In a mixture of bewilderment and tension, I picked up the phone and braced myself for what, based on my quick judgment, could only be bad news. I swallowed hard and answered. I could never have imagined what happened next. Because yes, it was Italy on the other end, and there was definitely big news for me. But it wasn't tragic. At least, not the kind of tragedy I had hastily imagined. Paolo Castellacci and Giovanni Moriani wanted to talk to me. They wanted to offer me a job to return to Italy, with the Sesa Group, which had paid for my master's degree and had since opened up an interesting opportunity for me to consider, etc., etc. Blackout.

The total unexpected

Communication was lost in that precise moment. Not that of the phone, but mine. Because that was the "total" unexpected. The thing I could never, ever have imagined. It interrupted a peaceful Irish afternoon in which, as always, I was busily working on my rise in a multinational company that I was learning to see as home; elbowing, pushing, and climbing my way through interviews. But this was no time to give in to a blackout. I came to my senses and started listening again. The group in general, and Computer Gross in particular, was about to change direction, riding a wave of change and expansion that was all about its first, historic acquisition. J.soft was the name of the company they were bringing on board.

Now, acquiring a company is no walk in the park. It's not something you can do on the spur of the moment. Companies have different histories, and each history carries with it the individuals who built it, brick by brick, and who have derived from that history a culture, a way of thinking, seeing, and doing that is unique to that company and no other. Two companies may resemble each other, but they will remain different and will never be identical. So to make them work together, it will take a lot of work behind the scenes to integrate them so that they operate in concert and support each other wherever possible.

To tackle a job like this, you can invent all the procedures you want, and you can throw all the money in the world at it. But first and foremost, you need a good driver. In fact, you need a whole team of drivers, working piece by piece to connect fabrics that were previously separate. Castellacci and Moriani wanted me to do just that. They wanted me to contribute to the integration of J.soft with Computer Gross, thereby increasing the firepower of the Sesa Group. That phone call, in essence, took everything I had painstakingly built over the previous six months (and perhaps even before) and blew it off the table where I was carving out my place.

Crossroads

That phone call put me at a crossroads once again. On the one hand, I had Dublin, an international setting, with ambitions to cultivate step by step. On the other, there was adventure, a risk, a challenging opportunity that only a madwoman would accept on the spot, and that was precisely why it appealed to me so much. Even if it came from a corner of the world that was infinitely small compared to what my horizons had become. And then, there was Antonio. He was my maternal grandfather, a man with a big heart and a not-too-distant past as a climber, the father of my uncle Giacomo, who was first of all a brother to me.

I loved everything about foreign countries, except for the distance that separated me from my grandfather Antonio. I wasn't just close to him, I was very close to him; and to keep a more tangible thread of the affection I felt for him, since I couldn't physically see him (at the time, video calls were science fiction), I discovered that in Dublin, right near my house, there was an active webcam, one of those that are placed in cities around the world and broadcast on the web. Every evening before going home, cell phone in hand (we did have those, luckily), I would stop by, dial his number, and stand in front of the webcam to wave my arm to say hi, so that at least he could see me. Whatever the weather, and preferably wearing something colorful, because the first few times he had trouble finding me.

On the one hand, I had a "home," lost in the mists of a green island but all mine, full of promises and inches to conquer, in a place full of people who were all different – from each other and especially from me – with stimuli that constantly fed the hunger I carried inside me.

The other option, in a certain sense, had a similar allure. Because the Italy option would bring me back home (without quotation marks), presenting me not with many challenges, but one big, attractive one, in a field that was not multinational but which piqued my interest, partly because I would be able to put everything I had learned the hard way to good use. The decision was very difficult, but on November 29, as always in a flash and with my answer ready, I set foot back in Italy.

Disoriented

It was November 29, and just like in the past, my assignment would start only two days later. On December 1, right on time, I walked into Computer Gross. The reluctance I had brought with me from Ireland had grown, and rather than feeling completely calm, satisfied and motivated, I actually felt nothing at all. I was strange, and I felt strange. Like a fish out of water, accustomed to the ocean and suddenly placed not in an aquarium, but directly on the shore. Then there was the shock of arriving and realizing that I didn't know anyone anymore. Because for a year and a half I had been a citizen of another world, compared to which Empoli seemed like a completely different universe, hermetically sealed by its culture and mentality.

Finding balance and perspective again was an enormous effort. This was also because every day I found myself having to deal with a world that, like it or not, had gone on without me and scattered so many of the images I kept in my memory.

All the friendships I had before leaving had followed this cruel logic of time. Many, as fate would have it, had done the same as me: they had left with no intention of returning. And they had kept their promise, unlike me. I was back to square one.

There's only one way to describe the beginning: disorienting. Work wasn't going much better. With one fundamental difference, however: the environment wasn't bad at all. Even though it was a small area, there was a young population that brought a certain enthusiasm and exuberance. It was also a fun environment, from what I could tell. I could only guess, really, because at first, not knowing anyone and coming from a climate (human, not meteorological) like Ireland's, where, as usual, I had become best friends with everyone within 24 hours, I objectively found it difficult to find my footing. In Dublin, at IBM, thanks to the fact that new recruits are often, by necessity, alone in a foreign country, the human climate is the opposite of the weather: open, sunny and welcoming. From the very first day you are embraced not only metaphorically, but physically. Considering that my previous experiences had also enjoyed the same openness, it was obvious that I would suffer from whiplash in a context that was not hostile but certainly foreign, and on top of that, in my own home.

During my first days at work, I invariably witnessed the same routine: while my colleagues went to lunch together, as usual, I stayed there like an idiot waiting to be invited. I would look up and a thought bubble would appear, which was the answer to a question that no one had yet asked me, and which always read: "Okay. I'll come to lunch, too, a little later." Or the unspoken question I wanted to ask: "Can you tell me when you're going to lunch, so maybe I can come too?"

Fists on the table

On top of all this, there was certainly another aggravating factor: having joined a company where, before being Francesca, and from the moment I walked through the door, I was and remained Moriani's daughter (and this was a big issue, which we'll talk about later), the one who acted like a big shot because she had a master's degree, etc. It wasn't immediate, and it wasn't spontaneous. But, with a little time in between, I eventually managed to make myself known for who I was, beyond my family connections, my academic qualifications, and the fact that I had come from somewhere else. In a way, things got better. But "only" on a personal level, in terms of relationships and people. Professionally, much less so.

Because, in the meantime, the dream sold to me that afternoon in

Dublin, that of driving integration, had slowly melted away like snow in the sun. What was left for me to do gave me no satisfaction. One thing after another, plus the aforementioned "existential" burden, was leading me inexorably to a single logical conclusion: enough was enough. After only four months, I increasingly felt lost in a tunnel and couldn't catch my breath or see the light again. It was at that moment that I banged my fists on the table and announced that, seeing no reason to remain stuck in that situation, I was going back to Dublin, and fast.

At that point, they came back with a different offer. Still in Italy, still in Empoli, and still at Computer Gross, of course. But as a manager. I had a new card to play. A risky one, though, so much so that Giovanni Moriani called me specifically to try to dissuade me. Don't accept it. Listen to me, you're too young; you'll get hurt. I listened to him, from the first word to the last. It was exactly the feedback I needed. Because I read it exactly backwards, as I had always done when someone showed me a closed door and warned me that it was a door that would never open, and that it was useless even to try. I accepted, became a Credit Manager, and immediately realized that I would soon start enjoying myself again.

Credit Manager, a how-to guide

First, however, I had to answer a question: what exactly does a Credit Manager do? As on many occasions in my life, this was not something I could improvise. So, once again, it was a matter of studying, growing, and above all, proving that with hard work, commitment, discipline and determination, things can be achieved. It was April 2004, and I would remain in the same role until September 2006. For over two years, I would spend fifteen hours every single day working and studying. I studied because I didn't have an answer to the question above.

So there I went, signing up for courses, buying and devouring books, taking notes, practicing, studying, and studying some more. The more I studied, the more I delved into the subject, the less confusing it became. The more I studied, the more I delved into it, the more I understood that Moriani, deep down, had his reasons for warning me. It was difficult work because it brought me to extremely demanding situations. Discussions where the only topics of conversation were money, cash flow, credit, and exposure. And taking the trouble and the direct responsibility of saying no to certain specific business orders, which I didn't think were reliable on paper but for which I then had to justify my decision to Paolo Castellacci himself.

Channels that perhaps had worked well in terms of credit up to that point, began to show cracks in 2004 because there was a storm brewing outside, with a crisis that was far more insatiable and merciless than mine, and was claiming victims among businesses as if there were no tomorrow. On the other hand, you had Castellacci who, confident of the company's solvency, indicated that we should proceed anyway. And you had to do everything possible and impossible to save the day, knowing that—right or wrong, based on trust or hard data—you can fix almost anything in a company, but once the money is lost, it's lost, and that's that. Because if you rely on the wrong partner and they don't pay up in the end, there's no chance of turning things around. It's enough to write a manual on stress, no doubt about it.

Those two long years before changing roles brought me to the symbolic weight of 45 kilograms. Yet they were very formative. I was worn out, but I had once again managed to strengthen my skills. And they were fantastic years. I was tired, but happy. The experience as Credit Manager took away my weight and sleep, for sure. But it also added an important contribution to my life. On the one hand, it deepened my acquaintance with David, whom I had already met in 2003 and who would not only manage the famous J.soft integration (which had been promised to me at the time) but would also become my partner (for fifteen years, until 2019) and above all, the father of my two children.

On the other hand, that season also gave me the "fertile ground" of a wonderful team, capable of giving me so much. And this—at the time I couldn't have known—would become a constant feature of my career. It's a fact: from then on, I had the gift of working with people who literally gave their heart and soul to what we decided together and achieved together. Looking back, it was precisely this rich experience of true collaboration with my teams that provided the compass that would guide me, many years later, towards different and diffuse models of leadership, to be developed and nurtured in organizations that were no longer siloed or closed, but open.

I am still deeply indebted to each and every member of that team and to that invisible bond – like a red thread – that has grown stronger over time because, despite having changed roles and despite the passing of time, it is still so clearly visible that when we meet in the cafeteria, we automatically stop to talk and catch up, thus keeping faith with a relationship that, even though the calendar says that twenty years have passed, was and remains exceptional.

Flexibility before flexibility

From 2004 to 2006, I gained experience in credit management. From 2006 to 2014 (and before moving to sales), I managed the relationship between Computer Gross and IBM. Those who worked with this team for a long time still let slip a "Boss..." when we meet, and I smile every time because I automatically think back to how extraordinary that group was. Extraordinary because they were "total" in what they did, in doing it well, in giving their all, from the first to the last. Extraordinary because, in a company that still had some way to go in terms of cultural innovation, we threw ourselves headlong into risky initiatives if we believed they were effective in terms of our objectives and if they made us work better. One example above all: we had created a flexibility laboratory ahead of its time.

I didn't care at all when and in what order things were done. Common sense told me I was much more concerned that things got done and that doing them led us where we wanted to go. That's why I didn't force people to stay in the office and work at set times. What mattered to me was that people were available to work when it was needed; actually needed, I should point out. And I asked myself: why work from 9:00 a.m. to 1:00 p.m. and from 3:00 p.m. to 7:00 p.m., when in fact, there was often nothing to do until 10:00 a.m., and, on the other hand, some tasks meant that we had to work until 10:00 p.m.?

Did we have small and large goals to achieve, which were shared and clear? We should focus on those and do everything possible and impossible to achieve the result, but not for the sake of form. Again: could it happen that certain commitments sometimes forced us to stay at home, even if we could still work remotely? Of course it happened. For me, it was nothing more than a realistic (i.e., in line with people's real lives) way of addressing what we could and had to do in practical terms, with a view to achieving, and possibly exceeding, goals that existed regardless of the time or place of work.

Now, all this would have been nothing more than an exercise in common sense. In those years, however, and in an environment that until then had strongly emphasized physical presence, it was enough to cause a series of headaches. And indeed it did. Especially for me, who received more or less veiled reprimands on several occasions because, for example, at 9:30 in the morning, some of "my" desks were "desolately" empty, since I had allowed those who had worked until 10 p.m. the previous day to arrive at 10 a.m. Or maybe they were empty because on that particular day some people were working remotely due to some family emergency—a broken pipe at home that needed to be repaired urgently, or whatever.

Time, on the one hand, and more intangible things such as "evolution" or "innovation," in a certain sense, have proven me right. What was once an exercise in common sense in its intentions and a laboratory of flexibility in practice has now given way almost everywhere (but not everywhere, yet) to remote working, institutionalized flexibility, and in the best cases, a sense of distributed leadership that is a common asset and heritage, healthily rooted in increasingly dynamic and open organizations. But even more than that, my satisfaction came from the results achieved by those teams made up of extraordinary, tenacious, stubborn people who were free to do their best and our best together.

Despicable me

Everyone is unique, there's no doubt about that. And I'm no exception! I've always been rebellious, otherwise I might not have been able to achieve everything I have. I'm disciplined, but in my own way. And rigorous when necessary. Sometimes reckless, why not? I'm someone who never gives up, who works hard and sweats. I love challenges: a few days ago, I climbed to the highest refuge in Europe, called The Margherita Hut, at an altitude of 4,559 meters. It was an exciting journey, a plunge into breathtaking views that only nature can create. On the way up I struggled, in this order, with altitude, mental and physical fatigue, and imperfect training. There were moments when I clearly thought I wouldn't make it. Then I dug deep, or rather we all dug deep. Determination and the will not to give up. I reached the summit and came back. The first thing I did was recommend the experience to everyone I met, to share the inspiration. I am someone who is inspired and knows how to share. Someone who hopes and persists. And yet someone who changes. Made of granite, perhaps, but only up to a point. Because life always has more nuances, infinite nuances beyond what you expect.

When I returned to Italy, when people got to know me and things started to take off, both for me and for the teams I coordinated, I tried to be the best friend, to include everyone, to get to know them. But I could also be a wild beast, and this must be admitted beyond any reasonable doubt. I would shout. I would get furious. I wanted everything to be perfect, down to the smallest detail, to the nth degree. I flew off the handle when people came to me with hearsay, without first studying it or bothering to look into it in any way to report back to me with a well-founded argument. I was determined, and my determination was iron. You could make a mistake with me, of course, and you could get away with it once. The second time, you had to face the music. I gave a lot of myself. And I expected the same in return. I was as approachable, friendly, and willing to listen as I was strict when it came to focusing. I didn't want to deal with people who took things lightly, just for the sake of it, without batting an eyelid when they made a mistake (which was fine, of course, but I didn't like nonchalance when it came to mistakes: embarking on something recklessly, thinking that if you mess up, it's not the end of the world...).

Things that change everything

That's how I was, and maybe even worse. Until I discovered something. Or rather, until something discovered me. Because there are things in life that don't just brush against you, don't pass you by, and when they arrive, they don't ask for permission. It happened to me when I became a mother; understanding what it means to become a mother.

There are things in life that stop you in your tracks, grab you and force you to look inside yourself, deeply and thoroughly; things that change you. Being a mother changes you: it shakes you up and challenges the very foundations of what you thought you were. Suddenly, you have to learn to listen more, to endure, to build yourself up, to nurture and consolidate a sensitivity that in other times and places you might even have mocked. And to rearrange the cards on the table, where your previous priorities take a back seat, and your children come first, always and in everything. To those who are not yet mothers or fathers, such a total change of perspective may seem apocalyptic. For me, it was a revelation, visceral and beautiful. Every revelation, however, to be truly such, comes with some kind of price to pay. My price to pay, the one that knocked me down and forced me to take a hard look at myself, perhaps to reevaluate, and certainly to rebalance the priorities that had I had kept until then and that kept me standing in the ring, in Italy and in a hundred other corners of the world near and far, was triggered by a timer that officially started on August 31, 2008.

Landing at Var Group

Without

Namibia is a place that defies our Western idea of a country. On the one hand, because it is a state that only recently gained independence, officially established in 1990 after first being a German colony and then a British Empire territory controlled through South Africa. On the other hand, because it takes its name from a desert and has a boundless expanse (over 800,000 square kilometers: just under three times the size of Italy) where nature has had fun creating the impossible, to then scatter just two million people (which is just two-thirds of the population of Rome, to give you an idea). All this territory, largely unknown and unspoiled, is occupied by a single plateau, a natural elevation that continues unbroken, exceeds 1,600 meters in altitude, and begins to slope only at a certain point, to the east, inland, fading into the Kalahari Desert, and to the west, when it touches the dark shores of the Atlantic, giving way to 1,600 kilometers of coastline, which here as well, are a total desert (the Namib, from which it takes its name). If it were a box, you could say that inside there is a bit of everything: red dunes and beaches dotted with shipwrecks, canyons and salt flats, lagoons and plains that only become such when it decides to rain. And then there are rock paintings as old as the world itself, German-style colonial buildings and geological formations in the shade of which elephants roam.

For someone like me who loves traveling, a place like this couldn't go unnoticed. A place where opposites sniff each other out, meet, attract each other, mix, and end up finding their own balance. More fragile than crystal, but perfect. A place like this is not (and can never be) a "simple" travel destination, not for me. Rather, it becomes something visceral, an existential question.

So, in August 2007, I plunged into a tour of Namibia. It was just as I had imagined it, true to the reason why I had chosen it, and even better, if possible. As such, it had "chewed me up" and finally returned me to Italy with a wealth of emotions. And then there were the people of Namibia. Tenacious and fearless, they lived peacefully according to rules that were much more essential than ours. Observing and getting to know them, life was stripped of the infinite shades of gray we are used to living with, reduced to an ancient and primordial game of black and white, full and empty. In Namibia, I saw women give birth in the middle of nowhere; relying on nothing; without teams of nurses, without a crowd of mid-wives, without any medical support, comfortable chairs, clean gowns, or providential epidurals. "No fuss," as nature intended. *Without.* I had seen all this happen, I had wanted to see it out of a hunger for knowledge, and from that exact moment I knew that it was something absolutely real. Raw, essential, authentic.

The chemistry of the brain

Seeing and knowing are things that move you deeply, change you, and alter your brain chemistry in a certain sense. They disrupt your equilibrium and then rebuild it in their own way. They force you to change your perspective, to reconsider what you have on the table, to weigh again everything you have kept on the scales until now. Sometimes certain things lie dormant, remain there for a while, and then reawaken when it suits them. What you see and know today will always, by definition, differ from what you will see and know tomorrow.

On August 31, the year after my trip to Namibia and that reality check, my first son, Diego, was born.

I was in the trenches, as always. I had worked until the day before, with the end of the quarter approaching, deadlines which thus became even more pressing, and so many, many things to do that delegating them, assuming they could actually be delegated, would have taken longer than rolling up my sleeves, gritting my teeth, and getting on with it. Then the time came, the rush to the hospital, labor, birth, and from then on I stayed at home. For exactly fifteen days. Because in mid-September,

I was back in the office, returning to work at Computer Gross in the morning, side by side with David, Diego's dad, and leaving after half a day. In short, the number of days of maternity leave I had taken was negligible (mentally, it was zero).

Let's be clear: I felt everything except indifference. Rather, I was walking on air, as unsettled as any woman who, after months of waiting, thinking, and fantasizing, finds herself becoming a mother. Intoxicated by the greatest novelty in the world, the one that, even after nine long months of waiting, finally arrives and completely changes the atmosphere. And it immediately makes you realize that there is no manual for being a mom (or dad): you have to sweat it out. And sweating it out is a huge privilege, a gift. A gift that fills you up with fuel, energy, and determination to do better and more than before.

In the long run, as a good iconoclast, I had also discovered that I was against the custom of leaving my children with their grandparents all day long. To take their place, since they were in charge of looking after Diego in the afternoon, I had set about finding a babysitter to look after my son in the morning, thus easing the pressure on the whole family. Everything was different, but it was working. We were creating a new equilibrium to replace the old one, which was naturally coming to an end, and I had a strong feeling that everything would work out in the end. I could feel it in my gut. But perhaps my new mother's intuition was wrong...

"Enjoy your baby..."

Diego was born on the last day of August and was immediately subjected to routine checks to make sure everything was okay. And everything was okay, according to the pediatrician who performed the first examination. Except for one thing: a slight heart murmur. In reality, it was nothing unusual or dramatic: sometimes babies are born with a small hole that exists and is real, but at the same time is absolutely minimal, because it usually tends to fix itself as the child grows. To be on the safe side, however, the pediatrician referred us for further tests, again at the hospital in Empoli.

So Diego was also examined by the head of cardiology. He confirmed the existence of the hole between the ventricles, but also that it was something completely normal and therefore very likely to resolve itself with time and patience. "Look, ma'am, just do one thing: enjoy your baby..." he said, sensing the obvious concern that a mother cannot hide, even with all the necessary precautions and reassurances. "The only thing I recommend at the moment is to come back here in a month for a check-up so we can monitor how things are progressing..."

That first month flew by in a flash, just like every first month as a new mother. And then the day of the check-up arrived. Same hospital, same verdict. Even after four weeks, the cardiologist found that the murmur was still there. The only difference from that annoying *déjà vu* was a dark note. There was blood flowing into his lungs. A lot, too much. The result: Diego was always suffering a little. So he wasn't feeding well; he wasn't growing. This was also why my son's skin was pockmarked like a tiny sausage, with lots of little spots that, in light of the new evidence, made it seem that something was not quite right.

It was worrying, but the specialist wanted to reassure me, confirming that nothing particularly serious had been identified.

In her opinion, the situation was probably related to the fact that Diego was struggling more than expected to find a balance between his heart and his lungs. It was tiring, but not dramatic, nor unusual. The conclusion was to schedule another check-up in a month. However, after a month, there were still no new developments. Same pockmarked skin, same feeding problems, same growth difficulties. At the check-up, I was even asked specifically if the baby sometimes tended to turn black due to the excessive amount of blood that was still flowing to his lungs. The picture was strange, and the cardiologist was beginning to feel confused.

Hell is a just another gray Thursday

As a result, she made an appointment for me in Massa, at a facility specializing in congenital heart disease. Today, that facility is the G. Pasquinucci Heart Hospital, but at the time, it was just "the Sacred Heart" to me. It was 100 km from home, neatly distributed along two almost perfectly straight lines, the first turning towards the coast from Empoli, and the second running parallel to the coast, passing Torre del Lago Puccini, Viareggio, Camaiore, and Forte dei Marmi. For many, it would be a beautiful, picturesque stretch of road, but for me it was just the road that would take us closer to the truth and to the solution we sought.

October 2 was a Thursday. We gathered our belongings and, once in the car, we drove all the way to that strange building, a piece of architecture that hints at the futuristic but is nestled among olive groves, carefully placed with its almost impossible shapes just a stone's throw from the green, wooded mountains of the Apuan Alps. The doctor we had an appointment with welcomed us, examined Diego, and gave him back to us. As I hugged him to comfort and reassure him, she explained everything.

From the results of the tests that had been carried out meticulously, repeated over and over again – because with matters such as these, there is no room for error and no room for discussion until the possibility of error has been reduced to zero – a certainty emerged from all the findings and cross-references regarding Diego. It was mathematical, rock solid; and terrible. The certainty that something was very wrong. The hole was there, but it wasn't where they had thought it was in Empoli. In other words, it was there, stealing space between the ventricles, but at the back. This meant it was invisible with the instruments used in previous examinations. Invisible, but it was there and, worse still, it was big. In such a scenario, the only solution was not to wait for it to grow out of itself, but to operate: open-heart surgery. David and I looked at each other, eye to eye, unable to blink.

On Thursday, October 2, 2008, in Massa, the weather was gloomy, tending toward cold, and the air was saturated with humidity. It was a rainy, gray day, perhaps a little oppressive for those sensitive to weather changes, but nothing more. For us, it was the apocalypse that heralded hell on earth. The world was collapsing around us because events were taking the only turn you had deliberately kept out of the deck with all your strength. The most dangerous, the darkest, capable of tearing hope away and shredding it to pieces. Because even though there was a glimmer of hope, and the difficulties were obvious, Diego was in every way like any other newborn baby, even better, in my eyes and in the eyes of those who had begun to love him and hope that everything, in the end and in some way, would turn out with a happy ending.

Pitch dark

For my part, I was full of positivity like any new mother, and I still had before my eyes a whole catalog of totally different conditions that I had seen around the world; less privileged, sometimes extreme, like those in Namibia. So, for me, for example, it was more than normal and sufficient for Diego to be weighed by the doctor during his routine checkups, and I considered it an additional and completely unnecessary stress to subject me and especially him to the endless sequence of weighing-feeding-weighing with a special scale at home. My universe, realizing that on the other side of the world there were women like me who gave birth to babies like Diego without any of these "extras," pushed me without hesitation to live everything more simply and with more serenity. But Diego, at that exact moment in his tiny life, was not in the same condition as everyone else in Italy or Namibia or anywhere else. He couldn't grow because deep down, deeper than we usually look, behind the surface, to be precise, there was something wrong. Something had come to light, and it was causing our world to collapse around us.

A hole between the ventricles requires surgery. And surgery here means open-heart surgery. For me, open-heart surgery on such a tiny body could only have one outcome, and that outcome was obvious. It meant certain death. I thought about it incessantly, as only a mother thrown into despair can do, but I couldn't say it. I thought it, and I tortured myself asking: how can such a tiny being, a tiny being that is mine, survive an operation like that? I thought it, but once again I hadn't reckoned with the world. Because seeing, knowing, touching with your own hands is something that changes everything, and changes you.

At that moment, in that place, on that hellish Thursday, October 2, my world suddenly went dark. Dark in contrast to my usual super-positive attitude. Dark over my indomitable energy. Dark over everything. Dark all around me, and darkness weighing down my legs. The doctor's reassurances were of little use: it was nothing serious, we could wait a while, also to limit and contain the risks as much as possible. I couldn't hear her. I was in darkness. A total eclipse of the heart.

"He can't"

Now, it was absolutely true that Diego was too young for an operation, especially one like that. He needed to get stronger, to let time pass to allow him to get to the operation in the best possible condition. He had to equip himself to resist, and we had to make sure he was ready. But we also had to equip ourselves alongside him. And while we waited, we had to deal with a monstrously long list of "cant's." Diego couldn't be in contact with people unless they were properly vaccinated. So vaccines for the whole family, vaccines for everything. He couldn't get sick or feel cold. So no closed or crowded environments, or anywhere that could pose the slightest risk to his still weak heart. He could no longer breastfeed because he wasn't feeding well. So I pumped milk like a madwoman to spare him the effort, and added a supplement to every bottle to help him grow. He had an avalanche of medications to take.

He had started swimming lessons when he was four days old, and now not only could he not set foot in the pool, but he also had to avoid going outside as much as possible, except for medical appointments. That's exactly how the first months of his life were; for him, and for us. There was little to do, nothing outside the usual four walls: at home, waiting for a day of total risk. For me, who had always sought, sifted, distilled, and found the beauty in things, making a virtue of necessity and, if necessary, running to the ends of the earth, all this was a double knockout, in which personal constriction was added to the worry for that son whom the cosmos had seriously decided to take away from me. Added to this was the burning surprise of having to deal, immediately and without any filter, with something titanic and unexpected.

What mother, father, parent could ever expect something like this? And even if you could somehow imagine it, how could you measure it in real life? It was too much, and I was reeling. So, on that same damn day of the Massa verdict, the first thing that made sense to me, the first thing I thought and did, was to inform everyone that from that exact moment on that cursed gray Thursday, I would no longer be working. I would stay home with my son; no more babysitters, no more everything else, because burdens of that weight need as many shoulders as possible. Once I had settled my accounts with work and devoted myself entirely to that relentless urgency, fifteen days of total depression began. It was pitch black, as if a flat, endless, inevitable, arctic night had descended upon us.

We had a whole season of regular check-ups in Massa to see how things were progressing. We followed a strict, tough regime that required a thousand little things, but in the long run, it didn't seem to be working. Diego wasn't growing, at least not as he should have been. At seven months, weighing just six and a half pounds, he was and remained very, very, very small.

A mother's heart

A mother's heart, like a father's, is a big thing. It has to be, because it also has to hold all the expectations, desires, and dreams of those who are still small, who have just been born and still have a long way to go before they can handle them. At the same time, however, that heart can become tiny and fragile, so much so that it risks breaking even with a simple gust of wind. When you give life to a human being, you pay a huge price in worries; that's the way it is and that's the way it has to be. But we also gain something extra. We discover energies we didn't know we had. We find within ourselves an exaggerated capacity for resistance, which doubles its strength because it hides something that keeps the life we have created safe.

The Massa verdict, and the whole season of periodic check-ups that followed, spent in watchful anticipation that something would start to change for the better, taught me in a completely unexpected way the art of patience, resistance, and perseverance. It was about clinging to the train with your fingernails, despite everything. It was about getting back on track, even when you didn't feel like it, pushing yourself relentlessly to keep going, day after day, until the end. It was a different kind of discipline from the one I had cultivated on my own. More complex, different, and completely new. But it was rigor, and I was going to play all the cards I had available.

We live in a sheltered world. Everything around us shields us from the harsh reality of facts; things we have built as defenses to limit as much as possible the brutal impact of what we cannot control. Every now and then, however, we get a taste of reality. It happens, and we don't dive in on purpose. It happens, and the effect is devastating. At the same time, all this has its own particular and decisive usefulness. Because it teaches you to put everything into perspective. When I started going to the hospital where Diego would eventually be operated on, I discovered that the withdrawal I felt inside, which I had imposed on myself and which was completely natural for a mother who had had something like this happen to her overnight, that very personal "tragedy," was little more than a cold for the world and the medical team.

Full stop

Because it could happen, and it happened more often than you might imagine from outside the walls of a hospital. Because the medical team was trained accordingly, and therefore knew exactly what to do to patch things up, to respond to all the pain that had sent me into a tailspin. When you broaden your perspective and try to look beyond your own nose, one thing usually happens in the end: reality begins to look different. A powerful alliance emerges that breaks down your loneliness. The hope you thought you had lost begins to sprout again. Then you learn to hang on. Then you start to fight back. Diego had a problem, but the doctors at that hospital knew what they were doing. They knew the what, the how, and the when. We could wait, and we would wait together, for the right time to face this challenge as well.

I was overwhelmed by despair, and I had every reason and right to be, but I hadn't really come to terms with the world yet. Which is vaster than you might suppose if you limit yourself to looking from your own backyard. And it has things in store, things to see, to learn, and to touch, which at any moment can turn the tables. Once I realized this, the darkness gave way to a new light. I put an end to the despair that had filled me, or at least I tore it from my soul and moved it to a larger container, where I no longer allowed it to be total, but forced it to become something absolutely relative, and remain so.

Once that was done, I decided to get back to work. At the time, we were working a lot with IBM, and partners of that caliber demand more meticulous attention than usual. Good will isn't enough, nor is ability or even "skill." You need something else: dedication. At the end of each quarter, as the deadline approached, we were plunged into a nightmare that reduced the rest of our lives, every single one of them, to practically nothing. The fall of the impasse slipped away, and with it winter and all of 2008. With spring 2009 just around the corner and a new quarter to close, what we had been waiting for too long finally arrived. We returned to Massa once again, and Dr. Murzi, who had summoned us specifically, informed us that the time was ripe to operate.

April 7, 2009

He suggested booking the room and the medical team for March 26. We were in a panic. Because when you're dealing with things of this caliber, no matter how prepared you think you are, when you find yourself face to face with them, all the precautions and plans you've painstakingly built up, consolidated, and set aside over time simply melt away like snow in the sun.

And then, there was something else. March 26 was not possible. Because there are things in life that you either follow through from start to finish, or you don't get involved. And when you find yourself between a rock and a hard place, you can't just listen to one side. To truly be there for the most important moment of Diego's life, both David and I needed to have a clear head and be focused.

We couldn't do that by March 26, and we couldn't deprive each other of the responsibility of being on one side or the other.

So we asked the doctor in unison if postponing the operation by just a few days would put Diego at risk. He replied, not without showing a hint of embarrassment, that there was in fact no risk, and we suggested postponing that crucial moment until April 7. To leave a storm behind us, together, and immediately afterwards throw ourselves together into that new fray. On the night before the operation, we entered the hospital, Diego and I together.

David and I had decided to ask the rest of the family, our grandparents, who were obviously eager to be there for the operation, to stay at home. We didn't want to focus on anything else: that day belonged to Diego and no one else, and for us, who had to manage everything, it was already extremely delicate. When the moment came, Diego was given a first injection to start the sedation. Then, in my arms, he was carried to the door of the operating room. It was the hardest moment of my life. I swallowed hard, waited for the door to close, and nodded vaguely as they advised us to leave the hospital to take our minds off it, as the procedure would take about five hours.

"Could you please come upstairs?"

Now we were completely alone, David and I. Two floors down, the hospital exit, a newsstand to buy a newspaper devoured in a hurry so as not to think too much, a totally sterile walk, breakfast nearby. Then back to the hospital, we stayed at the bar waiting for the time to pass. The five hours were still far from over. The wait was hard, the hands of the clock too heavy to slip away in an instant. Words and chatter were kept to a minimum. Then, a ring from nowhere. Not even three hours of waiting. "Could you please come up to the ward? The cardiologist would like to talk to you..."

Darkness, act two.

Why were they calling us earlier than expected? Why did the cardiologist need to talk to us? I didn't even have time to formulate half a hypothesis before my legs were already flying up the stairs. Two flights of stairs in an eternal second, my heart pumping blood into my ears and all that waiting, both past and future, wiped away by a gust of wind. When I arrived at my destination, I was the one struggling, my lungs squeezed by the effort and the rest of my body trembling with agitation. Dr. Murzi looked at me, distraught: "Madam, what's wrong?" "Look, you called us well ahead of the five hours you talked about, please be patient, but I'm a little worried..."

"No, look, maybe I didn't explain it clearly: it's true that the entire procedure lasts five hours, but my part is very small, because I had to close this hole between the ventricles, and while I was there, I saw a small hole between the atria and took the opportunity to fix up the whole heart a little. From there, I checked that the heart started properly again, and then I left the others to finish."

The procedure lasted five hours, BUT that was the total time. This meant that during the first part, Dr. Murzi did all his work, but so did the rest of the team, who once the surgery was over, would suture, fix everything up, and take Diego to intensive care.

I was jumping up and down. Because I was suffering from the crazy rush. Because I was a bundle of nerves and suppositions. Because I was still waiting for the simple, mathematical, and incontrovertible outcome of the operation. Because a second little hole was discovered, and more worries arose. Because Dr. Murzi had fixed everything, and there was a huge sigh of relief. But I was still waiting for the final outcome... It came immediately: the operation was a complete success. With Diego in intensive care, we decided it was finally time to notify our family. We called our grandparents, who were waiting anxiously to ask us if they could come, because, being human, they also wanted to be close to us at that moment, which finally put an end to the suffering for both us and their grandson.

"Lucky"

A step back... When the pediatric cardiologist, in a very detached manner, first informed us that Diego would need open heart surgery, I shifted my posture to steady myself on the chair (I was standing, holding Diego in my arms). Perhaps I tried to cling to it. Not out of anger, but out of despair. Not out of fury, but because I felt like I was literally sinking. I had never fainted in my life, I had never been the type, but at that moment I think I came very close. The doctor noticed, looked at me, and asked with what seemed to me to be exaggerated aplomb: "Ma'am, what's wrong?" I quickly gathered my wits and replied, "Doctor, look, you're telling me that my two-month-old son needs open-heart surgery. I think that feeling a little overwhelmed is understandable, don't you?"

She took an interminable second to respond. She lowered her eyes, then raised them again and looked for mine: "Believe me, ma'am, you are a lucky mother." I shook my head, taken aback, as she continued: "Not everyone hears that the problem can be solved with surgery." That comment struck me as odd, a kind of consolation prize. I kept thinking that I could feel and consider myself anything but "lucky." That "lucky" was something else, something very different. I was wrong, and wrong in a big way. I was wrong, and in the ten days I spent in the hospital with Diego after the operation, I had absolute and indisputable proof of that.

With Diego in intensive care in Massa, David and I had very limited privileges to visit him, as we were only allowed access to the ward for one hour a day. It was an agonizing experience, but it was also part of the grand scheme of things, the kind that turns everything upside down and forces you, in one way or another, to look at everything from a broader perspective than you would from your comfort zone. In intensive care, I saw things that literally knocked me off my feet. They made me reevaluate everything, without exception.

Something's trembling

With the operation finally behind us, in the midst of our convalescence, we happened to spend Easter in the hospital, which fell on April 12 that year. I was there with him, and a few meters away from us was another little patient, hidden behind the medical team that was crowding around, bustling about. They did all this and more, but in vain, because at just eleven years old, that child was bidding farewell to this earth. Eleven years old. On Easter Sunday. Just a few inches away from us. Things like this happen all the time. Inside and outside hospitals. Things like this have the power to make you tremble. And to reshape your life, including the problems that, just a few minutes earlier, you insisted on hating and couldn't stand. Afterwards, everything changes; tastes and colors change, and the way you face each day changes. Problems, troubles, difficulties: grains of sand in an infinitely larger game.

That same Easter day, Dr. Murzi came to see Diego. He came because my son had electrodes in his heart, installed as a precaution to facilitate the resolution of any irregularities in his heartbeat, considering that in the days leading up to Diego's visit, his sinus rhythm had not returned. That day, however, everything was back to normal, at least for us. So the electrodes could finally be removed, and that doctor, whom I consider a hero, gave up his afternoon rest to come over and take care of that, too.

The Heart Hospital is anything but a traditional hospital. Above all, it is more than you could ever imagine from the outside. It is "its" people, who fight silent battles every day to ward off death, never giving an inch, with the courage and dignity of those who must live with whatever happens next. It is a doctor who fixes hearts and does not hesitate for a second to get up from the table at Easter and come and remove wires. It is a wise pediatrician who, when she tells you that you are a lucky mother, does so with complete knowledge of the facts.

So, before you leave and close that heavy door, you go find her, find her and tell her with the same frankness she used with you that yes, she was absolutely right. That you are a lucky mother, because by spending a short but intense part of your life within those walls, you have managed to understand what the real misfortunes of life are, how they strike and what damage they can cause. And you are still there to tell the tale, and above all, your son is still there, and now you can start again.

Diego had his operation on April 7. With the full presence, total support, and all the hope that David and I carried in our hearts. It was the day after the earthquake that devastated L'Aquila, and there the earth continued to tremble, and would do so until evening. Something was trembling here too, but this time it was to drive away the nightmare forever: with the operation a complete success, and all those harsh lessons learned the hard way, we went to reclaim our lives. In mine, beyond my passion for work, Cesare, our second son, would soon be arriving. I wanted them to have the chance to grow up together, without too many years between them. To understand each other better, to work as a team, and to support each other.

What a child can teach an adult

And so it was. Shortly after the end of Diego's troubles, I discovered I was pregnant again. It was the beginning of a beautiful month of May in 2009, and I would carry Cesare and his 4.3 kilograms with me until February 4 of the following year. Cesare (who would eventually become a jack of all trades, including playing *Yesterday* barefoot on the piano and, in middle school, doing a PowerPoint presentation on a famous woman who fought for gender equality, focusing on me) was born in the evening, as usual, after a day in which, until just an hour earlier, I had been at home working. I left, rushed to the hospital, and had an extremely quick delivery. While Diego had difficulty breastfeeding for objectively and completely justifiable reasons, Cesare stopped drinking only when he was full. And this time nature, fate, or whoever was in charge had been more merciful. I insisted, and Cesare grew.

I insisted because my center of gravity had shifted. Because those two had changed my life, each in their own unique way. One had laid the foundations, the other had consolidated them. Together, they had taught me to look at problems in a new light and had reshaped my priorities. Better still, they had pushed me to find space and ways to balance my passion for my work with a whole new equilibrium, which is what happens when you become a mother, of course, but in my case it went much further than that. In the mid-1990s, Paulo Coelho wrote a novel called *The Fifth Mountain*. In it, he included a sentence that goes like this: "A child can always teach an adult three things: to be happy for no reason; to always be busy with something; and to demand with all their might what they want."

For my part, I think I did pretty well on all three counts, always striving to give it my all. But at the same time, I think there's a fourth item missing from the list: a child can teach an adult to feel life again for what it really is. After Diego and Cesare, my world took a different turn, and as it turned, I found myself noticing, really noticing, a whole series of things. Things like sensitivity, the ability to listen, the ability to understand if the other person actually had needs that were different from those I was used to encountering and considering. And then there was the constant questioning of everything. Becoming a mother, becoming one in circumstances such as those that befell me, profoundly transformed me.

Today, it's a head-to-head battle on my desk. On one side, there are Diego and Cesare, who are growing up and whom I see becoming, not without a great deal of pride, exactly what I hoped they would be; infinitely better than those who brought them into the world. On the other side is my great passion, the one that makes me look at what I do with the objective difficulty of labeling it with something reductive like "work." I say head-to-head, but both you and I know very well that, in comparison, Diego and Cesare win hands down. Because giving life to a human being changes you, and from that moment on, that human being always comes first; which is also perfectly normal. But in the life I am telling you about in these pages, which is my life without filters and without excuses, there is not much that is flatly normal (and then, what really is "normal" anyway?). And that primacy, that final result, was not at all a foregone conclusion, if we take a step back and broaden the frame a little...

When I grow up

My arrival at Var Group came just after a decade spent at Computer Gross, where I started on December 1, 2003, and, step by step, year after year, I eventually found a certain peace of mind. Between 2012 and 2014, I enjoyed, more or less consciously, that comfort zone where I had my team, my activities, my acquaintances, and everything I needed to breathe again and recognize that, yes, taking stock and drawing a line, I was doing fine. It was a period of grace, so much so that I was almost thinking about having a third child. Then certain events occurred. As you have already read a few pages above, much of my work at Computer

Gross revolved around "my" IBM business. It was tiring, complex, and entailed a lot of responsibility. Yet every time, it became one of those games that leave you tired but happy.

At the beginning of 2014, though, something changed. IBM decided to sell its entire X-Series server business to Lenovo. It was a significant portion of the business we did with them, which suddenly disappeared. It wasn't a tragedy for the company, but it was certainly a radical change. For me, however, it meant a drastic reduction in the playing field. I needed answers, and those answers concerned the immediate future. So, half-jokingly, I went straight to the source. My source, the person I reported to directly, was Duccio Castellacci (who is still CEO of Computer Gross, as well as the son of the founding partner Paolo Castellacci).

I found him together with Alessandro Fabbroni. They looked at me and, as a joke, I threw a comment and a question on the table: "... Now we have to decide what I'm going to do when I grow up. I mean, what am I going to do, given the news about the X-Series?" That's all I said; nothing more, nothing less. Between the lines, joking aside, there was something more. Without the work on the X-Series, I didn't have much left. I couldn't stand working with the brakes on, and they knew that perfectly well. So a decision was urgently needed, and a decisive one at that. My not-so-small provocation came at a particular moment in history. It was period in which meeting after meeting was called to try to respond to a sense of urgency, heightened by the realization that, somewhere in the Group, as a whole, something was not running smoothly.

It was in this context that my shot in the dark resounded. After which there was a moment of total, palpable silence. Then I made my move. I repeat, in the totally naive manner of someone who is there more to joke than to be serious. "Maybe it's time for me to lend a hand at Var Group..." I had thrown out what was only a joke and therefore, once said, I would forget it immediately. But I realized that something was strange because of the lingering silence. I quickly tried to lighten the mood, as it was meant to be a joke and I wanted it to remain so, especially at such a "differently simple" moment. "Guys, I'm joking, I don't want to leave, let's be clear..." It was the absolute truth, in all honesty and transparency. I was happy at Computer Gross (perhaps too happy); leaving wasn't even an option in the back of my mind.

"… Pulcinella told the truth"

Maybe three days went by, then Duccio slipped into my office, closed the door carefully behind him, looked at me and said that he wanted to talk to me about something. Laughing and joking, Pulcinella told the truth, as in an italian traditional proverb. But with one big difference. I really had been joking. Except that, unbeknownst to me, at that exact moment in history, the senior partners (whom Duccio referred to with a more colorful term, "*the dads*," meaning Giovanni Moriani and Paolo Castellacci) were already seriously evaluating my transfer to Var Group. Obviously, I knew nothing about it. I hadn't been informed in the slightest, and I was the only one in the dark. Duccio and Fabbroni's silence in the face of my jokes spoke volumes: in a totally unconscious way, I had touched the raw nerve of the moment.

I was perplexed. I hadn't considered it and couldn't consider it, especially given the state of grace in which I had been sailing until then (apart from the X-Series). I remained so throughout that day and the next. At least until Paolo Castellacci came to see me. He wanted to officially notify me that my transfer was currently being considered. I called Giovanni and asked him why on earth I hadn't been told anything. He replied that, not knowing how I would take it, he wanted to finish the assessment first to understand whether and how to tell me. I hung up.

Five minutes passed and the phone rang. It was Paolo Castellacci again. Between one "I'm sorry" and another, he informed me that, for the good of the Group, they had concluded – almost *in absentia*—that my transfer to Var Group was the best option. There was one condition, though: the transfer would only go ahead if Var Group offered me a role in line with the professional growth I had demonstrated with my skills after years of working on the front line.

The train and Chinese water torture

There is news that doesn't hit you all at once, as a train would. It arrives in installments, one piece at a time, like drops of Chinese water capable of hollowing out a stone. This was precisely the case, because only five minutes after Castellacci's call, Moriani shared with me the Var Group organization chart that they had already put together. An organization chart in which I occupied the position of Director with responsibility for sales and transactions. I would therefore work exclusively on vendor management and sales. However, looking at the figures, this represented something like 95% of the Group at the time. There is no response to such an offer. You don't choose whether to accept or not; you take it and go. I replied that I would make myself available to the Group, and in February 2014 I started turning the page, scrapping my comfort zone.

According to the senior management's plans, this transition was not supposed to take place until April, at the end of the fiscal year. But at the beginning of February, as Sales Manager, I was tasked with going through all the Computer Gross partners with whom we worked closely to draw up rebate plans that would be valid for the entire year (a marketing strategy used to increase customer engagement through incentive offers). I was supposed to stick to this, start and finish my round, and then move on peacefully. But something felt very wrong: it seemed totally unfair to visit partners, get involved in their business, and set up strategies, only to then go and work, practically overnight, for what was effectively their main competitor. This scruple became a lump in my throat that wouldn't go away, so I went back to my seniors, told them about what I felt was an unprofessional course of action, and concluded by saying that if my move was a done deal, it should be closed immediately, without waiting for April.

They agreed, and the first thing I did as soon as I left the room was to call my team to announce the news and start thinking about how I should behave at the annual event that IBM held for its partners: a whole week in Las Vegas for Partner World, which today is called Think.

I started with my work at Computer Gross already formally behind me, and my job at Var Group not yet begun. Hybrid, if you will. I left together with Giovanni Moriani, so that he could take advantage of that break to tell me about Var Group. Because, in all this commotion, I didn't know a thing about Var Group. Incidentally, the distance between the headquarters of Computer Gross and Var Group in Empoli is measured in meters. Two buildings facing each other, but between them, especially for me, there was a whole galaxy of distance.

When you think you have all the answers, life changes all the questions

I knew nothing. I had never even climbed the stairs or walked through the corridors of Var Group. But starting the following Monday, that would be my destination. That Monday arrived. I got in my car and headed to work, trying to keep a nagging question at bay: what am I going to do now? It was a new, strange, momentous journey; even though it was the same route I had taken every day. I stopped along the way, took out my cell phone, and poured all the confusion that was consuming me into a Facebook post, squeezing it and compressing it into a simple sentence: "When you think you have all the answers, life changes all the questions."

Between the end of 2003 and the beginning of 2014, I had unknowingly settled into a comfortable situation, in complete control. Now the fun was over. I had to go back and face a totally different environment. Where should I start? And how? And, before that, where should I go once I physically entered Var Group? One thing I knew, though: Simona Pelli, whom I had known since I was little, worked at Var Group as Marketing Manager, thanks to the group dinners where everyone brought their whole family. I parked, called her, and asked her the huge favor of saving me from embarrassment by picking me up at the front desk and showing me around, even if just to get an idea of the layout of the offices. Going in alone would have been a leap into the dark for me; which, if you think about it, is terrible, but also extraordinary. Because you don't expect a Moriani not to even know what the company headquarters looks like! We simply take it for granted that DNA works miracles and that we automatically feel at home.

For me, and for the eternal struggle against stereotypes that has always raged within me, it was something totally unnatural. At the same time, however, I was amazed at how wonderful it was. Because that not knowing, not having seen, not being able to find my bearings, drew a line behind which, beyond the last name I carried with me and everything that "Moriani" could humanly mean in that place and at that time, there was, always and unconditionally, Francesca. Simona rushed over, listened to me, and escorted me in that very first encounter with the new world. My office was a sort of storage room, and it remained so for the next few months. No complaints at all, at least not from me.

The problem arose more for the rest of the Var Group population, considering that those narrow walls that enclosed a small space, in the end and by some phonetic magic, became the perfect sounding board for my already not exactly faint voice. So, I would speak, the sound would echo throughout the ether, and outside there were those who would pass judgment. "Moriani's daughter is here," "the shouter is here." Which, on paper, was true, but scandalously incomplete. Because it left out a dense and considerable piece of my personal history, with that decade spent fighting just a stone's throw away from there, at Computer Gross, but it didn't even go into why I actually shouted and demanded so much from everyone who worked with me, and first of all from myself, because before I was a Moriani, I was and remained Francesca, with the added effort of making myself seen, recognized, and known as such.

Shout

My arrival at Var Group was not entirely smooth. Before I showed up at the office as the Managing Director, there was the usual leak that made everyone on the teams I was responsible for at least a little scared. Perhaps it was just a normal reaction: the new and unknown always arouses some concern. But for them, in fact, I was not completely new, nor was I completely unknown. Apart from my last name – and this was confided to me directly by the people concerned at the time, with a transparency and honesty that I could not fail to recognize and honor – I had a very specific reputation.

The shouter. A tough "Computer Gross beast," filled with an aggression that those who saw me at work considered an end in itself. For me, however, it was the rough determination to fight and flail about in order to assert myself for who I was, me and me alone. Francesca. To tear off, once and for all, the labels of "daddy's girl," "woman," and "too young." All elements added together in the minds of those in front of me, resulting in an immediate and awful shortcut in their thinking, which automatically judged me, convicting me without any evidence as someone who couldn't understand a damn thing she was doing.

That's why I always had to make a huge effort to express my ideas much more and much more strongly: just to be taken seriously. Over time, I realized that this harsh approach wasn't the right one. I could learn to achieve the same goal in different ways. But in those circumstances, I didn't have the time or the alternatives to explore.

Demand

I shouted, of course I shouted. And I demanded (and still demand) a lot. As I said, first of all from myself. Because I find it unfair and senseless that, when faced with something that is considered a goal, and therefore worth achieving, people don't bend over backwards to get there. That at some point they come up with more or less convenient excuses to slow down, stop, or get distracted.

This was my landing at Var Group. The more I tried to silence the stereotypes that people wanted to stick on me, the newer ones emerged. One above all: everyone tended to assume that, since I came from distribution, I would want to continue along that same path. Perhaps prioritizing relationships with vendors over other things, such as building a value proposition. Well, that wasn't the case at all. In fact, I no longer felt comfortable in distribution, mainly because I was becoming increasingly aware and convinced that it was finally time to change pace and scale, to do something that would bring greater value to the market and the end customer. I had one thing in mind: to build a real, solid, concrete, and recognizable service offering.

It would take time, it was no joke, and I had to start from scratch. But it was worth it, and I had to begin somewhere. I lived in the paradox of being alone (in fact) and at the same time being all too well known (but due to stereotypes and distorted or incomplete interpretations).

The strength of the "gang"

The people I could honestly say I knew at Var Group could be counted on the fingers of one hand, and the number dropped dramatically if you moved from knowing someone to having a relationship with them. Many were old acquaintances, whom I had met when I was still a child, thanks to the group skiing trips I went on with Giovanni and Sandra or occasional company events (dinners, parties, etc.). They were old acquaintances, sporadic at times, with people with whom I now found myself sharing experiences on a totally different level, that of work, at an age, adulthood, radically different from when we had originally met. This also weighed heavily on my difficulties and expectations.

Sometimes, however, the best glue is discomfort and suffering. I found people who, like me, at that precise moment were suffering in some way, or perhaps, like me, felt a void that needed to be filled. All of us, myself included, felt a great need: to build something new, outside the usual dynamics that created conditions of deprivation for us, to build all this together and cling to it tenaciously. It was an alliance, an alliance of redemption, if you will. This has remained an important theme for me from that moment on: working at any level, we can and must build alliances to support each other's vulnerabilities, coalitions that create space to welcome each other for who we really are.

There were people who had seen me work before, who had taken that extra step to understand me, scratching beneath the surface, and had discovered that they were in tune with me, with my perhaps strange and particular way of being, of doing business, of living my private life. With some of them, a deep friendship developed. It was a strong bond that tied together a handful of just over a dozen people, regardless of their role in the company, their specific place of work, or their length of service (which, in the vast majority of cases, was not reflected in their age, considering that we were all very young at the time). Twelve/fourteen friends like this, close friends, aligned, scattered throughout Italy out of a total of six hundred colleagues who at the time made up the entire workforce of Var Group, represented something formidable. And in addition to being good for the soul, they helped us understand and deal with everything that was looming on the horizon, even before it had time to materialize and happen.

For me, in that "out of place" year of 2014, a gang like that was a breath of fresh air, and it accompanied me through the long months leading up to the fateful Kick Off 2015 in Viareggio, with which I opened this book. Not that my schedule was empty, quite the contrary. Because with the whirlwind I had in mind, the company had to be prepared first. And so I worked toward that goal: for example, I facilitated intergenerational change, taking responsibility for the retirement of many over-70s and paving the way for the arrival of younger resources.

Profane ritual

And then there was Giovanni-centrism. When I set foot in Var Group, the company's alignment with Giovanni Moriani was tangible. For his part, he had always been opposed to hierarchies and organization charts. You could say that he lavished autonomy on everyone, even if, as a good *maître à penser*, he was "condemned" to being the target of constant requests for support or advice on everything. Giovanni demanded a lot, but at the same time he never shied away from his open-door policy, his willingness to receive, listen, and talk to anyone. In hindsight, this openness was probably excessive. In fact, it jeopardized the very principle of highly autonomous organization that inspired him and ended up being overwhelmed and crushed by the deadly aura of his charisma. A charisma, moreover, that was neither declared nor flaunted, but totally unconscious.

Giovanni Moriani was and still is a super humble and super helpful person. He doesn't get carried away and never has. I have no excuses; he has no pretensions. In defiance of all those "great company leaders" who, in one way or another, end up showing off, walking on human skin, commanding others only because their only weapon is their desire to impose themselves. Giovanni, on the other hand, just needs to be heard because he is competent. Competent not because of his role, but because of his personal qualities and experience. And so everyone at Var Group ended up depending on him in one way or another. Even though that was not his goal, nor had it ever been. The hold he had over others was like the sleep of reason in Goya's painting: dangerous, because it ended up creating "monsters." This is a lesson I would begin to learn later: the path to autonomy for those who work with you requires an empty space that every leader must cultivate by literally "not speaking." As Captain David Marquet, author of the wonderful book *The Leader Ship*, says, "When we give people instructions, we create dependency; when we give space to their intentions, we create autonomy."

The endless crowd of people who, at the beginning of my assignment at Var Group, came to me for advice on anything and everything was a reflection of the same profane ritual. She's Moriani's daughter? Let's go to her; she must have inherited some of his charisma.

This is what it was for the people of Var Group: an established secular ritual. For me, it was the source of a new Herculean task: to uproot a stubborn tradition, in which there was a figure halfway between an oracle and a confessor on one side, and on the other a crowd of people wandering around asking, "What do I do about this?" in order to be reassured with an opinion ("I would do this, this, and this...") that in their eyes was an inescapable divine law.

Dad, Giovanni

It was a great comfort, humanly speaking. For Var Group, in my humble opinion, it was a supreme tragedy. Because it undermined the company's ability to evolve, leaving six hundred people more or less comfortably seated in their cocoons, depriving them of the opportunity to test their abilities, their sense of responsibility, and the contribution they could make to the growth of the organization. A giant bottleneck had been created, that was undoubtedly fascinating but people were unaware of what it represented.

Giovanni used to say, "Go for it! 100% autonomy." The problem, however, was that we didn't yet have the right tools to make decisions independently, a transparent and shared system of agreements that would enable the community to take independent action. Autonomy was an aspiration; more than that, it was a calling, but it was not matched by organizational clarity or a structured way of responding that was useful to people. Giovanni welcomed everyone, always. And everyone went to him with the same question on their lips: "Is it okay if I do this?" Without tools, all he could do was explain step by step what to do. And in this way, he created a habit, a widespread custom, according to which when you didn't know what to do or how to behave, stopping by his office was the perfect shortcut to finding the missing solution. A thousand answers ready, zero responsibility.

I couldn't stand it, I couldn't accept it. And I was going to do something about it. I would do it myself, on my own initiative, because I could and because I looked up to that charisma with admiration, of course, but I would never have dreamed of drowning my own responsibilities in it, too. I had to do it because I was Francesca before I was Moriani, something I never forgot at work. I had to do it because I had never allowed myself the freedom to call him "Dad" at the office.

Even though, every time I mentioned Giovanni, whoever I was talking to always ended up asking me the same question: "Giovanni who? Giovanni Giovanni?" "Giovanni Moriani," I replied peremptorily. And, in response, I got the snide remark: "What, you call him Giovanni?" Over time, it had become a little theater, where the script always called for the same performance. I would spread my arms, roll my eyes, and reply with complete naturalness, "Of course, what else would I call him?"

It always happened. Except, of course, with the group of a dozen people who knew me inside out: the "gang," which in the meantime, was becoming more and more united. Friendship, passion, spontaneity, trust, transparency, and emotion. Together, we felt like an increasingly strong team, we had each other's backs, and we did amazing things, both at work and outside the office. Months passed, then years. And we had no idea that 2019 would bring with it an unexpected turning point and a thrilling reshuffling of the cards...

How was Francesca the entrepreneur born?

Inches and teamwork

> The inches we need are everywhere around us. They are in every break of the game, every minute, every second. On this team, we fight for that inch. On this team, we tear ourselves, and everyone around us to pieces for that inch. We claw with our fingernails for that inch. Cause we know when we add up all those inches that's going to make the difference between winning and losing... Now I can't make you do it. You gotta look at the guy next to you. Look into his eyes. Now I think you are going to see a guy who will go that inch with you. You are going to see a guy who will sacrifice himself for this team because he knows when it comes down to it, you are gonna do the same thing for him. That's a team, gentlemen...

Whoever wrote Al Pacino's speech to his team in the most difficult, dramatic, and delicate moment of *Any Given Sunday*, in my humble opinion, must have had a moment of total inspiration. A direct line to God, to destiny, or whatever you want to call it. Because, aside from the endless interpretations of coaching, this film reveals a couple of key points that are absolutely essential to the story I am telling you in these pages. The first is inches; my inches, the ones that took control of my steering wheel and led me, bit by bit, on the path we would eventually take. Well, I sweated those damn inches in the early years, but also in the first few months that followed that extraordinary landing at Var Group.

The second is the team, the "gang." Because those few inches that inspired my future and that of Var Group owe an enormous debt to a small number of people whom I trusted implicitly, whom I respected deeply and, if you will, with whom I had formed a kind of chemical bond, and ultimately, a friendship. It was a group that worked wonderfully, regardless of role, seniority, or geography. It worked because it cultivated a sense of unity all its own. A passion that was as strong in the office as it was outside. They were people who were as determined as I was to get the extra inch, as it was never enough. They fought for me, knowing that when the time came, I would do the same for them. Shoulder to shoulder, always. With them, thanks to them, for them, I was able to keep going; and survive difficult times, which was by no means a given.

In 2019, I had them on my side, my role as Director with delegated powers, and the fact that I had spent years working tirelessly to significantly grow the services side of the business. The rest—the applications business, the set of relationships with Sesa, acquisitions, and so on—was still very much Giovanni's domain, who instead played the role of Chairman with all the relevant powers in his hands.

Quantum leap

In 2019, however, the wind began to blow in another direction. A totally unexpected direction. Giovanni fell ill. He began to have problems with his legs, a constant numbness that quickly turned into pain and spread to his feet. It was strange and deeply distressing to see him like this. As a colleague and as a daughter; remembering the iron sportsman I had always seen in him. Soon Giovanni had to focus on this, to put his mind completely to a problem that he not only did not expect, but above all he couldn't quite define. He couldn't give it shape, clear boundaries, or a rationale.

He couldn't have done otherwise. And, in fact, he disappeared, completely; first mentally, then physically. So, overnight, without that oracle to whom crowds of people turned for advice on everything, life turned on a blender and catapulted me into the role of Chief Executive Officer. At first, I was working behind the scenes—because the official appointment would only come in 2021—and I found myself filling a huge gap that had suddenly opened up in one of the most critical areas of Var Group, with no gradual transition to such a big and cumbersome responsibility.

The quantum leap in that difficult year taught me that there was not a sea, but an entire galaxy between saying and doing, as the proverb says. And this was even before Var had embarked on its current trajectory. Then, it threw me into a new season of difficulties, as I juggled a thousand new responsibilities that were raining down on me, even more people coming to ask me things and many other things to study, learn, and put into practice. Because it's true that I had been with Var Group for a while, but there were aspects of the world of applications with which I was not yet familiar, because I had never had the need to get my hands dirty, as that had always been Giovanni's territory.

Sooner or later, it will work against you

In that season of alarm, worry, and urgency, my life began to change a little. For example, having my mind elsewhere, work commitments, the constant concentration required to stay afloat amid the stormy seas, being CEO on the one hand and a mother on the other, ultimately led to the end of my relationship with David at that very moment; but in a very amicable, peaceful way, so much so that we love each other more now than we did before.

Change, at least a certain amount of change, is natural. The point, however, is that when big things change, things that shake you up inside and affect the way you see the world, the first people to notice it are not those who happen to pass by, but those who care about you. Those who have learned to see you for who you are, for the unique way you do things, who share more or less intimate aspects of themselves with you. When my change began, I knew I had to let go of many things because there was no alternative, because it was necessary and, as such, right.

Perhaps, being directly involved, I didn't even have time to understand exactly how much I was changing. I didn't, but the gang noticed it right away. And not everyone took the new turn of events very well. So, with them unhappy to varying degrees and I, on the other hand, busy taking note of their discontent while at the same time holding the reins of a company that was growing also at my personal expense, I realized that Giovanni had never really gone away. Or, at least, that at that exact moment he was coming back into my head and my gut with something he had said to me some time before, which I hadn't paid much attention to until then.

"This very close, somewhat carnal relationship you're building with people, I don't think you'll be able to maintain it. Sooner or later, it will work against you." That flag raised in unsuspecting times, which for me was just a point of view and little more, was proving to be well-founded. It now seemed like a kind of prophecy. But it was only half a prophecy. Because, in fact, the discontent I felt tangibly in my circle stemmed from a unique relationship, built together, to which we had contributed by adding each brick, and which we had cultivated and cemented together. It was a close relationship that gave so much and now demanded just as much in return. But as far as I can tell today, that bond had in fact turned against us. Or rather, it was beginning to abandon us, albeit in different ways, and loneliness had become the prevailing feeling.

I felt abandoned, unable to count on Giovanni and occupying a chair that can make you feel surprisingly uncomfortable, taking up a lot of time and sapping your energy. Everyone who was part of that group felt abandoned, some more than others, because in my constant rush, busy schedule, and preoccupation, they could no longer find someone to listen to their work problems, make plans for the weekend or holidays, or even just spend an evening with. For those who, for example, had tirelessly cultivated the healthy tradition of eating out on Fridays and then moving their brainstorming sessions anywhere but the office, simply dedicating themselves to clearing their heads to see how much better their ideas would be when they expanded their horizons, my constant absences were, without a doubt, a source of suffering.

I couldn't get organized, and I ended up becoming the permanent absentee, the one who wasn't there. The whole gang suffered, including me. Disappointment, however, is a strange and very personal thing, and the way you experience it also determines how deep the suffering can become. There were those who took the blow particularly hard, and even ended up leaving the company.

Months ago, during a dinner celebrating Var Group's tenth anniversary, I was able to experience firsthand, through their memories intertwined with my own, the depth of the break they had to deal with. The sudden cutting of an umbilical cord, which cracked a perfect circle that was a source of pride for them, that made them feel different from others and that, from one moment to the next, fell apart for reasons they could not grasp, generated somewhere distant from them. Taking the floor amidst raised glasses and clinking forks, I wanted to tell those who were part of that group, even those who are no longer with Var Group, that without that gang, I would never have made it through those early years. That I owed them a debt of gratitude deeper than any disconnect, because in them, despite their different characteristics and ways of acting, I had found the right support to face challenges and difficult moments, without ever forgetting that life is something special and wonderful.

Ten years

In some ways, years later, we in the "gang" still miss something about that period that was all ours. The freedom to move around, to act, living in a simpler, smaller company. Those memories, which for many are tinged with regret, have the same mythical flavor as when we think back to our childhood, to the simplicity of a golden, distant world where everything was less worrying, less risky, less complicated, and you could lose yourself looking at the sky without the pressure of your conscience telling you that you're wasting time, that it's late, that there are tons of things to do, and they all have to be done, invariably, right away. The patina of time then makes everything seem more romantic, blurring the contours and smoothing out the rough edges, because deep down, everyone needs beautiful stories to remember.

Today, the intimacy of that time is no longer there. Because many paths have taken more or less unexpected turns, and trajectories have often diverged. Some took other paths sooner than others. There are those who have continued to grind out the miles together, like Mirko, who has been by my side from day one and whom I consider one of the most important people in this organization (even if we have our fair share of arguments from time to time).

Ten years ago, I was alone; without tools, without weapons. A woman, and Moriani's daughter to boot. I was the one who didn't understand anything about what this company did. The whole group, without exception, didn't just help me, they super-helped me. Many of the ideas I brought with me to the stage in our Kick Off events came from them, from aperitifs, evenings out, and that extraordinary, wild ability that we were blessed with to let ideas flow. My damn inches, the ones that shaped the career choices I made over time, also come from there; that's where they were born.

Some paths diverged, as I said. At the same time, new and very strong bonds were formed that are here to stay. With some people (I mentioned Mirko, and I could say the same about Alessandro) I still attend leadership team meetings (which we call Var Talks, as we will see later) and above all, I still feel a bond that is certainly professional, but also goes beyond that. It is a bond that has matured, leaving behind the strong, sometimes excessive intimacy that characterized the gang. It is a new bond, more mature, perhaps more "managerial," but no less empathetic. It is more mature because we have matured, and our way of working as a group has evolved accordingly.

Firestarter

A trigger is the factor that sets off a series of effects; the fuse that sets the firecracker off. That was me. I set things in motion. I ended up in the middle, I put myself in the middle. It had always been that way, from when I organized children's games to when I went without hesitation to meet the new kid on the ski team, to when I mediated between the group to find something to do together. For serious matters as well as for fooling around; for complicated, thorny issues and for fun ones. At the first company parties, if I wasn't the first to hit the dance floor and start dancing, no one else would. I would get started, and the collective wallflower moment would end.

For me, it was completely natural. I didn't do it to show off, get noticed, or be admired. I didn't have that kind of goal, quite the contrary. But by dint of doing it, always me and invariably first, by dint of breaking the ice and overcoming hesitation, for me and for others, that role had begun to stick to me, with all the expectations of those who, in the end, knew that mathematically, at a certain point, Francesca would step up and take the lead. You can do it once, twice, a thousand times. But you can't always do it; it's inhuman, for you, who find yourself with a sword of Damocles perpetually hanging over your head, and for those who, in the end, willingly or unwillingly, end up settling in.

They will never know if, at some point, you don't step aside. If you don't allow things to evolve naturally, and have other people take the initiative, everyone to contribute. Of course, if you decide to put an end to that habit, it will be your fault if they feel disoriented. It will be your fault, at least for a while. Because sooner or later they will understand and roll up their sleeves. They will understand and get things moving again. And at that point, you will no longer have guilt to deal with. You will have contributed to the beginning of a new and better period. A season of widespread autonomy and responsibility. Perhaps "at the time," when I was putting these lessons together, I wasn't fully aware of it. But they would be things that I would carry with me, that I would cultivate and try to develop, spread, and make flourish.

"Did you know we're doing this, and it's working?"

A new way of acting, carried out in groups formed in a different way. A way of being sparks, triggers, fuses, leaders if you will, in a distributed manner. Without always depending on the usual trailblazers. Without being dependent on gurus, sages, more or less unconscious masters of thought, who end up being a bottleneck for the entire company. No more closed groups, but open organizations. No more centralized leadership, but a single culture of leadership spreading like wildfire in an environment where things happen on their own, driven by people who are not afraid or hesitant to get behind the wheel and go. In the future as I see it, in the future I want to see, I walk around with a big smile on my face, because things happen at Var Group. And I smile because they happen and, more and more often, I know little or nothing about them.

Big, important, promising things, which I am once again unaware of, but this time in a good way. Things that I didn't want, didn't want to, and couldn't even get involved in and "babysit," because they run themselves. And things happen that I know something about, that maybe at the right time I planned and see go by as finished, but also completely new things that I know nothing about. Things that people stop me to tell me: "Did you know we're doing this, and it's working?"

Because I am a Moriani, but before that and above all else, I am Francesca. A rebel, outside the lines and the box practically since birth. A woman and a mother who used to be a screaming beast, elbowing her way through and demanding to be known and recognized. I don't want, with all my heart, I don't want and have never wanted to be an oracle that people depend on.

I like to win, I like it the way most people do, but at the same time I appreciate stumbles, setbacks, missteps, and failures. I respect them for what they bring to light, for what they can teach you, and for what you can draw from them and use in the present or in the future. This is who I am now, and tomorrow I may be something else. I weathered the perfect storm of my early days at Var Group, I left behind the storm in which I had to steer the ship in Giovanni's absence—first in the field, then also on paper—and I made peace with myself by dedicating myself to looking back and reflecting on the great failure of my small but great "gang." Then, finally, the time came for me to take stock and shake things up big time...

(A certain) Idiosyncrasy

All these great upheavals were connected in some way to a feeling, even more than a conviction, that had deep roots in my own upbringing.

Let's go back a few years. While I repeatedly immersed myself in the multicultural bath of that house which was in fact a colorful cosmos amid the mists of Brighton, the master's program I was attending at the time exposed me to a lecture in which, in addition to organization charts, there was extensive discussion of hierarchies. With the model company depicted in the classic pyramid slide: the CEO at the top, then the general director, and below them a neat and expansive cascade of managers of something, managers of something else, and so on, down to the roots.

A standard pyramid; sterile, minimalist, stripped down to the bare bones so that the entire company could see and understand it. Nothing more, nothing less. A pyramid that triggered everything in me just by looking at it. My eyes crossed. My stomach churned. And something began to screech loudly in my head. I hadn't been out the night before. I hadn't eaten junk food for dinner. And I wasn't coming down with the flu. That ample, visceral discomfort had another cause, much simpler and more subtle. Exaggerating, perhaps, it could have been called idiosyncrasy. That's what happens when you're allergic to something at the slightest contact, and that something is capable of triggering an exaggerated revulsion. Hierarchies and organization charts didn't make me break out in hives or feel nauseous. But in that class, I was discovering that, in my mind (and not only mine), they were something viscerally wrong. They didn't make sense to me, and I couldn't come to terms with all those people who decided this, who had delegated authority to others, who had no authority at all, and so on. It was a hierarchical torment mixed with organizational torment, with all those big and little boxes, lines running from top to bottom, as if it were an anonymous family tree of an amorphous, impersonal power, duller than the ungenerous climate of that part of the world.

The "rules of the game"

And it didn't end there. Because then they started explaining the "rules of the game" to us, the etiquette of power whereby it is not just good, but excellent practice to keep as much distance as possible between managers on the one hand and "the people they command" on the other. Because personal involvement can have a negative impact on team management, you must know. They had to tell us, they had to spend time and attention on us, because at the end of the day, it was an MBA, and since the dawn of time, an MBA has taught people how to become "managers with a pedigree"; illustrating both written and unwritten rules. They explained, and my headache grew. They also insisted, with a whole series of practical examples.

England is the home of the pub, not as a business but as a culture. A pub is not just a place to go for a drink, but a slice of history, a way of meeting and sharing, of forming a group. You find all the locals at the pub. Everyone goes there: young, old, politicians, revolutionaries, the working class and the governing class. What must a manager—who is surely a man—do to measure himself against the institution that is the pub and come out on top? He can invite all "his" people, of course. He must open a tab, of course. He must buy the first round of pints, obviously, and join in the toast. But then, once that's over, just like Cinderella in the fairy tale, he has an absolute and unpostponable duty to slip away. Gone, without even leaving a glass slipper behind.

Because the team must feel free to express itself. And it can only do so in the total absence of those in charge; who, for their part, gain credibility because they avoid showing themselves to be vulnerable, which would expose them to the risk of no longer being followed at work. I had followed the reasoning up to a point, and perhaps I was already beginning to feel a little better. But when it came to the moment of escape and the pair of reasons that were sold to us as if they had been written in stone, I confess, I was at a loss for words. What sense was there in a boss—and I repeat, conceived as male—running away, because by staying and doing what everyone else did, he risked no longer being taken seriously? How much beer would he end up drinking and how could he possibly make a fool of himself? And what could those people possibly have to do or say to each other that was so secret while drinking beer in a pub? Were they plotting against the company, the world, the establishment, freedom?

Where was the logic? Nothing made sense to me, and it still doesn't. Because I thought, and still think, I must say, that if you are competent and credible, if you really know what you are doing, and if we happen to find ourselves having a drink together in the evening (or a meal, whatever you prefer) whether in England or Korea, Oslo or Wichita, there is no reason, not a single reason, why you should lose credibility. That thought, once the lesson was over and the amazement had faded, did not completely disappear from my mind. The screeching stopped, but that flash of insight, sudden and profound, remained with me. Bad rules for a game that smacked of the old. I carried that insight with me back to Italy, more or less dormant, until it reawakened on its own.

Babylon Galaxy

In truth, at Computer Gross, this criterion of proximity had always been implemented to some extent. In the sense that, in the daily hustle and bustle and on balance, there wasn't all that much distance between me and the others, let alone one codified in the English way, so to speak. We were a team, bound by friendship; we were many things together, at the same time. So when I arrived at Var Group, that same vocation for proximity followed me and continued to play a very important role over the years. This was also because at Var Group, that attitude of "zero distance" found an absolutely favorable environment. And when you plant a seed in fertile soil, it usually takes very little time to sprout.

This fertile ground for a culture of proximity beyond organization charts and hierarchies was grafted onto an ecosystem, that of the Group, which was already highly organized by companies; companies that, over time and one after the other, had entered the perimeter through a series of acquisitions. And which therefore retained a certain degree of autonomy, which could be more or less pronounced, but was always autonomy nonetheless.

Now, from someone who gets stomach pains at the mere sight of an organization chart, from someone who has always kept her distance on the field close to zero, one would expect that, finding herself in such an environment, she would automatically feel as if in Nirvana, or almost. Not at all! As someone who was and remained a rebel, in the end I had to work extremely hard to regain control; not to have personal control over everything, but to build an organization that was effectively *in control*, capable of the dynamic balance that our uncertain and complex world now requires. Because autonomy is right, sacrosanct, but like all things—as popular wisdom teaches us—too much of it is too much.

Let's take another step back. I wasn't even CEO yet, and Giovanni was still firmly in his position. It was 2016, and an alarm bell had started ringing constantly in my head. It was the same alarm I had heard in Brighton, but this time it was sounding for completely different reasons in that galaxy of companies that lived and operated within the Group, each with its own distinctive characteristics, the result of the path each had traveled up to that point. But their identities, rightly autonomous, went beyond that in some respects. And that "beyond" was a problem for the whole Group.

The straw that broke the camel's back was actually visible right from the start. In plain sight, but somehow hidden, like a flaw in your home—a chipped piece of furniture, a mismatched set of glasses—that you end up not noticing because it's right in front of your eyes. Each company had its own logo and continued to use it: orange brands, yellow brands, green or pink brands, and then dotted ones, with shields or little hearts on top. A Babylonian fruit salad that created a 'Harlequin effect' whereby, apart from the pyrotechnic impression, the only thing that was not understood, that did not "come across" and that there was no need to convey, was precisely what could have worked to the advantage of all the companies: their belonging to the Group.

That's why I got migraines again. That's why I embarked on a patient and laborious process of homogenization. Incidentally, that process bore fruit the following year, in 2017, and rather than a veiled suggestion, as far as I was concerned, it was a monolithic imposition: having the same brand to start showcasing the Group, to convey the idea of a Group, above all to feel part of a group. So, years after that lesson in pure suffering, I was also discovering that the absolute, in itself, however fascinating it may be on paper, must always face the litmus test of reality. Which is always a question of "how" rather than "what." A question in which the "how" brings with it concrete actions, and concrete actions, in turn, also lead to failures and scars. Because the "how" always has to do with people, and since reality is absolutely varied, and so are people, the recipe must adapt accordingly, at least a little.

Managerialize

Over time, I would have other opportunities to test this theory. One of the most significant was related to hierarchies. In the early days, Var Group was not managerialized. Imagine it, if you will, as a gathering of pure entrepreneurs. But even here, things did not go smoothly. So, little by little, it became necessary to introduce a certain degree of structure. Perhaps we made mistakes. In fact, in a managerialized organization, those who have recently been appointed managers are constantly looking for one thing above all else: hierarchy, because they need to have a clear picture of the organization, with the boxes above and below them, in order to position themselves on the chessboard and thus define their scope of action.

If you are fully aware that you are on a ladder where the top is the highest rung and the bottom is the lowest, and you also know that your position occupies and "is worth" exactly one of those rungs, you will naturally tend to aim for the rungs higher up, those that separate you from the top; starting with those just above you. As you scramble to climb, however, you will realize that you are not alone on that ladder, which is actually a company, an organization, a group, etc. There are other people in different positions from yours, also trying to climb to the top. Then you will realize that among those who are puffing and kicking, there are also those who would like to climb up to your rung or, worse still, those who start from your place because they have the same goal as you.

At that point, you will have discovered competition for internal positions. This is the dark side of managerialization, because those who live to compete do not know how to collaborate. Instead, they are obsessed with standing out in every area: beauty, decision-making, ability—the keys to earning the next rung on the hierarchical ladder.

I had hated hierarchy and organization charts with a passion, only to find myself committed in a certain way to defrosting them and putting them to use. But it wasn't over yet. In order to patch up old and new problems, I saw even worse trouble on the horizon.

The only rule is that there are no rules

We couldn't afford to have a group torn apart by silly internal wars of vanity, because sooner or later we would have ended up paralyzed, unable to work together, and ultimately the economic and financial results would have suffered. At that point, I took all the hierarchies and organization charts and threw them in the trash. At the same time, I left a convenient door not just open but wide open for another resounding blow.

Navigating without hierarchy and doing without organization charts, personally but also for the entire Var Group population, wasn't so bad; quite the contrary. Partly because, in the end, a strict, rigorous, and meticulous organization chart wasn't necessary, since the top lines were known, and as long as they were able to coordinate well, they worked without any problems. Partly because Var Group was going through a period that, seen through today's eyes, would be considered ancient history. It was a much smaller group than it is now, more manageable in practice, with a series of activities that were still fairly limited in scope. Put this way, simply scrapping boxes and pyramids was fine. But the "fine" was purely contextual, and we didn't know that yet. It fit more or less perfectly for that specific period. So, all that was needed was for the planets to shift just a few degrees to throw off the balance, and for a puff of wind to blow and make it sway.

All it took was a puff, and that breeze capable of making us shiver began to blow unfailingly in 2019. With the advent of Covid, the breeze became a hurricane, and once the pandemic was over, the hurricane was followed by a tsunami. Paradoxically, all that turmoil was not a curse for Var Group, but quite the opposite.

With Covid behind us, the company found itself literally catapulted into a trajectory that made it grow out of all proportion. Those were the years when my particular obsession had a first name and a last name (actually, two), and even a title. Reed Hastings. Erin Meyer. *The only rule is that there are no rules*. Which, in addition to being one of the "commandments" of *Fight Club*, is the title of a sensational book that Hastings and Meyer wrote to tell the story of Netflix, its culture of reinvention, and that concise phrase that served as the title of the book and constantly echoed in my head like the best of mantras. Caught in this loop, I looked at the world through those lenses. And I was convinced that everyone had the sacrosanct right and freedom to take the initiative, precisely "without rules."

Another blow

I didn't know it, I couldn't imagine it, but the abyss was close, we were heading straight for it, without even passing "go," and even without our sails up, if possible. Because that "you have complete freedom to do"— dropped into a company in absolute and dizzying growth, which as such was becoming increasingly large and heterogeneous, and which in all that luxuriance was also filling up with areas that were neither black nor white, but a growing infinity of shades of gray—well, that "freedom to do" became not an invitation to constructive freedom as I understood it, but the equivalent of parachuting the accounting department into the jungle or onto a desert island, without tools for survival and with the imperative to find their own way as best they could.

I had dreamed of Netflix, but found myself in a mass *Cast Away* situation. I repeat: I had not anticipated this possibility at all. I had simply applied something that felt right to me, that the cosmos suggested was right (Netflix book in hand), and above all, I had been overly radical.

I needed something dramatic to open my eyes. And that something revealed itself in all its power at the end of the year.

A Christmas party with a meeting, which people attended with a certain amount of *moral suasion* on my part, as I had repeatedly insisted on a few necessary points. The first: stop talking about "legal entities" because it created separation between people and made it seem like we were lots of different companies without a common goal to share. The second: stop talking about "responsible persons" (what exactly are they? Do we need responsible persons so that others feel less irresponsible?). And again: no more organization charts, it is forbidden to show organization charts in public and, above all, it is for-bid-den to show organization charts in public. With the accompanying hissing threat of an immediate public flogging for anyone who even hinted at boasting about their hierarchical position.

It hadn't even crossed my mind that, paradoxically, the "rules" I was sprinkling around were not rules at all, but *prohibitions*, all of them. And, even worse, that I had gone overboard with the list of "don'ts" without suggesting what could be done, what was "allowed," what remained to be done. With premises like these, the event hadn't even started yet and it was already saturated with pressure. And it would explode in my face, because whoever took the stage, people whose abilities I would have staked not one but a thousand lives on, would start to flounder, stumble and sweat profusely, not knowing what to say, and above all how to say it, without running afoul of one of my prohibitions.

Basic tools for the whole Var Group

All things considered, and with hindsight, I would have been surprised if it had been any different. Because, in that series of prohibitions that allowed no exceptions and that we accepted without question, not really knowing why, people no longer even knew how to present things, how to represent them, how to explain them. They were constantly on edge even with words that were actually part of their natural vocabulary, but which they knew they couldn't use because they would bother me. So they sweated, they stumbled over their words, they had no choice but to muddle through, babbling and achieving little. But their discomfort was nothing more than my own failure, mine and that of the Netflix-lined blinders I had stubbornly put up against the wind of change.

It was there that I realized I still didn't understand. I hadn't fully grasped the lesson. Faced with that theme, which started out as if it were an absolute ode to freedom, but instead ended up in the worst kind of imprisonment. We had an organizational problem to solve. And we had to get to work, either on our own if we felt up to it, or with the support of those who already had solid experience in this area if we didn't (which is what ended up happening). We had to deal with it as soon as possible, because if we didn't, we would throw away everything. And it didn't all deserve to be thrown away. The "Spotify lesson" – to bring up another company often cited for its organizational culture, the one that had struck me on the road to Damascus – pointed in the right direction. Freedom, however, thrives on limits, and in order to find the key and get our bearings, we also needed tools to create, share, and use to the advantage of the autonomous initiative of those we were pursuing.

We had a problem of chaos. The idea of removing hierarchies and organization charts and throwing everything out the window without establishing rules of conduct had caused organizational chaos at Var Group. And to get out of such chaos, you need instructions. Not too many, but a few basic ones. Our rules of chaos, designed to generate not absolute order, but "our order": an orderly chaos, if you will. The only ones valid and applicable for people with a healthy dose of madness like us.

Paradox

The market exploit I mentioned a few pages ago was neither figurative nor metaphysical. It was not a philosophical issue, nor a perception due to some state of bliss. It was made up of numbers, figures, and results. It was *hype* in the flesh. In the flesh, albeit technological, and it led Var Group to a leap in scale that was reserved for those who had somehow managed to do without a retro, monolithic business approach, in which points of contact with the market are few, immovable and always the same, in favor of a literally opposite strategy, where old silos and ancient compartments are overcome because of a voluntary choice to play in an agile, adaptive way, with platforms on which products and services travel that, instead of responding only to themselves, talk to each other and to the market, reflecting it.

This was the "technical" picture of Var Group's growth. An expanding organization that looked very promising in terms of numbers. But at the same time, paradoxically, as soon as you looked beyond the business, you couldn't help but notice people who were paralyzed, struggling painfully because they were drowning in chaos. Because they had no idea who could decide what, when, and in which areas. And so, between one futile attempt to swim in quicksand and the next, they ended up choosing not to decide at all. It was a company of dogs running around in circles, only to end up chasing their tails. It was 2021, and we had left the most dramatic phase of Covid behind us; but the darkest night was still ahead of us.

When I managed to regain control, understand where we were heading and what would happen if things didn't change course, first among ourselves and then with respect to the market and our client companies, a total upheaval began, which has been going on for several years now. We opened a construction site, choosing to enlist the help of Kopernicana, a company made up of crazy people, just like us. We have no intention of closing that construction site (to which many others have been added over time), not yet. Not even after the many questions I have received over time and continue to receive from time to time, all of which focus on why we are embarking on this adventure, given that "in the end, we are doing so well in terms of numbers..." It is legitimate to ask, and those who ask me that exact question are right, in their own way. They just forget to look at the big picture; a picture in which it is true that the turnover and EBITDA are those of a company that is doing very well. But it is also true—and our recent history teaches us this and is here to remind us—that this is not enough. Because, in my very humble opinion, "doing well" also means something else. For example, it means dealing with people who are happy, who are able to express themselves within the company, who bring their skills to the market in a calm, confident, attentive, and focused manner, and who therefore create satisfied customers.

In front of the mirror

Financial results aside, or rather together with and through financial results, my concern was (and still is) to have happy people at work. Put like that, it can mean everything and nothing at the same time. What does it mean to be happy in a work environment? For me, it means being able to live it. Finding yourself doing something you enjoy. Something that gives you satisfaction, that makes you realize that, at the end of the day, you can stand in front of the mirror, look yourself in the eyes, and admit to yourself that yes, today you did something good, and you know why. When I worked at Computer Gross, I would sometimes come home late at night with the distinct, palpable feeling that I had been away for a lifetime, with fourteen straight hours of work behind me. Tired, exhausted, eating quick dinners, the moment that whirlwind stopped spinning, I was always hit with the same bunch of questions; unavoidable, relentless, clear as a razor.

What did I do today? Why did I work fourteen hours? What good did I do to anyone, to work myself to death like this, like a dog? These questions were legitimate, and less obvious than they might seem; less obvious, above all, than a final rhetorical question that, as a corollary and out of exasperation, invariably popped up to close the whole series of silent, intimate questions I asked myself: *Wouldn't it have been better if I had packed my bags and gone to Africa to work for a non-profit organization?* The questions were not obvious; they came "from within" and represented the gentle way in which my conscience tried to make me see reason. The problem, however, was not the questions. It was the answers. Answers that I did not have, or that perhaps I was not yet ready to give myself. Because, at the end of the day, I couldn't see a real, rational, solid reason to shut myself in the office for more than half the day, stay late, and go straight into standby mode (not falling asleep, but shutting down) before the alarm went off the next day, for all that frenetic hustle and bustle.

Asking yourself questions in the mirror is a harsh test. It lays you bare, and when you are bare, the scars you have are more visible. It is because of the answers I could not give myself at the time, in the dim light of evening and in front of the mirror, that I am now pushing so hard to convey to people the concrete reality of what we are doing at Var Group. Because I want the mirror to forgive them for everything that, at the time, it did not let me get away with. Because we may not be the best company in the world, but we certainly aim to be the best company *for* the world. When I say that our goal is to contribute to the economic and social well-being of the countries in which we work, I say this with full awareness, and with respect for a commitment that is measured in deeds. Because it involves "doing" and has an entirely different impact (and quite different figures) than the simple and trendy "saying."

From writing on the wall to something that happens

The training we offer people is based on this same assumption. It aims to turn this proclamation into a tangible reality, transforming words on a wall into something that actually happens, creating more aware citizens and contributing to the well-being of the society in which we live. One of our advanced training activities is aimed not only at developing the future leaders of Var Group, but also at benefiting them personally. The course lasts ten months and culminates in the assembly of a project work, the scope of which is decided by those who are to carry it out, choosing from a short list of topics, and then working on its implementation not in just any context but in the living reality of Var Group. It is therefore not a simple theoretical exercise in a "laboratory" setting, but rather a chance to think about and plan a specific future, imagining it based on the exact reality of the present.

At the end of the last edition, a colleague presented her project to us, one focused on fatherhood. I opened it and looked at it. Then I looked at it again, and again, and again. The more I looked at it, the more extraordinary it seemed to me. I asked for permission, got it, and went to HR. "Look at this, isn't it cool? Can we do it?" Because today, paternity leave in Italy is only ten days; and almost no one takes it, partly because there is not enough awareness about it. But knowledge is there to be shared, to become common heritage, not to end up hidden or buried in a drawer. What's more, in addition to sharing it, we can aim higher; by replacing, where necessary and precisely because it is necessary, what other entities (the "national economic system," whatever that means, aliens, Superman, etc.) are unable to achieve.

The idea, in this specific case, was to extend leave to one month, using paid allowances. A three-year trial period with one month in the first year, two months in the second, and three months in the third. HR looked at me, narrowed their eyes as if focusing on something, and replied simply: "Cool!" Which was already a great start. But it didn't answer my second question. It was cool, but was it feasible? Now, in an identical situation, assuming that absolutely identical situations can be created, in a company X, there would most likely have been a series of precautions and arguments that, boiled down to their essence, would have been nothing more than variations on the same theme: "Why should we do it?" Translated: if the idea is to do it to help women, in reality it is more of a support for those who do not work at the company, because the leave is for colleagues who become fathers, and not necessarily fathers and mothers who work in the same place.

Average result in company X: nice, very nice, but not worth the effort.

Result at Var Group: let's do it, and let's do it quickly. Because we will be doing good for families and for our country. We will contribute to making people happy, and in doing so, the company will also be a better place. Happy people in better places will (also) help generate higher profits. And when evening comes, tired but happy, we will look in the mirror and not only feel but know with certainty that we have done something good for society as a whole, even before thinking about our company's accounts.

Purpose and transparency

All of this is because a company—even if we often forget it today – also has a social more, whether conscious or not: to create a supply chain that is not only an end in itself, but capable of making as many people as possible feel good. You don't achieve a supply chain like this just by instinct or a sinister ability to make money. You achieve it if you can combine instinct, ability, and desire with something else; with the ability to find a purpose in the work you do, a reason to oppose the severity of the mirror, your "happiness." And in being able to do all this at the right time, without adulteration, calmly; without having to force yourself to be miserable. I've seen plenty of people who arrived in the morning bent over double, staggering, and the first thing they said was that they hadn't slept all night because this and that and the other thing had happened the day before, to then go on with a whole catalog of troubles. That's why I sweat and work extra hard, so that between the people and the troubles that constantly haunt us (myself included, you know enough about my story by now), there is at least a barrier, a safety net. And may that barrier be the best possible, the happiness of knowing that you do things for a reason, that that reason produces facts and not words, and that you have an extra purpose, at work and as a person.

The reason why; happiness, purpose, but also chaos. The fight against organization charts. "Complete" freedom, that is raw and without rules. All of this, including the setbacks, taught me a lot. It was a reality check and a learning experience. It also allowed me to give weight and importance to other things. Transparency, for example, and the absolute need for sincerity. Let's be honest: in our world, there is always a tendency to hide things. You don't always tell everyone everything; because it's tiring, difficult, and uncomfortable. And anything would come to mind except... spitting out the truth as it is. When you have a problem, when there is a problem, and that problem may be yours, a group's, or everyone's, practicing sincerity often becomes a kind of Russian roulette. With ourselves first and foremost.

The eternal struggle between good and stereotypes

All the scars I carry with me from the organizational setbacks that led us to where we are today at Var Group and what we are doing for Var Group can be traced back to a basic lesson: transparency. For me, this is something fundamental, a new chapter in my very personal battle against stereotypes. Financial data is protected by two thousand passwords, because, for heaven's sake, it must be protected, but then we are surprised that, since it is not shared for security reasons, people end up not having a clear idea of exactly where we are going, how far we can go, and where the line is beyond which initiative becomes dangerous. By overcoming the stereotype that information must remain "at the top," transparency can become a tool for organizational effectiveness that enables initiative and entrepreneurship across the entire Var Group. For years, I was a shouter, a woman, Moriani's daughter, etcetera, etcetera, etcetera. You know this well by now. Perhaps, however, you are still unaware that I also had a reputation for being a chatterbox. Because, people's opinion was that I couldn't keep a secret. I just couldn't do it, and compared to many stereotypes that got in my way, perhaps this one was even justified. But the issue here was another, deeper, and radically different. Why do we have to have secrets? Is it a legal obligation? A moral imperative? Is it prescribed by a doctor? Is it cool because it adds a touch of mystery? Seriously? Think about it: it was something that, once again, had endless points of contact with that strange lesson I learned in Brighton: the inviolable law of distance. Because those in charge, even if they offered the first round of pints, invited everyone to the pub, and paid the bill, then have a full, absolute, immediate obligation to leave at the end of the first toast. Because custom dictates that they leave the stage, that they close the stage, so that the rest of the people can breathe again. Safe, behind the scenes, enjoying life as it really is, and stop pretending.

The stage versus the wings. Doing one thing in front of everyone, and something completely different behind the scenes. One thing because it's convenient, the rest because that's how it really is. These are theatrical poses, which are fine for masks. In business, there are no masks. With masks, the company gets nowhere. In a company, you have to be yourself, just as you are at work and at home. You are there, as you are, and you have to be as happy as possible.

Masks

Even stereotypes, stripped down to their bare bones, are masks. Except that you don't wear them yourself; you make other people wear them. Worse still, you stick them on other people. And they are particular, treacherous masks that distort and suffocate. In many companies, there are still lots of people who are forced to wear a mask when they go to work. A mask that sometimes even includes a tie, to be clear, and to refer back to the story of my first Kick Off. But it can also be anything else, big or small. For example, once ties were no longer required ten years ago, we also had a problem with... shirts.

Enrico is still our Group legal advisor. He grew up here just like me (he joined in 2015, at the age of thirty, in response to a sort of "experiment" designed specifically to address the absence of someone like him), and was also part of another group, the historic one I have referred to in these pages as the "gang." He is from Pisa, with a turbulent and eventful youth and a politically charged past, which is reflected in a few tattoos he got at the reckless age of eighteen. Enrico is a friend, a colleague, a great professional and, if you will, a bit of a historical memory. But at the same time, for a while he was also a damn scared person. Because he felt he could do anything in his head, except show even a corner of the drawings he had on his skin. Obviously, he didn't come to the office in shorts, so the problem was limited to his arms.

His solution was always the same: shirt buttoned up, sleeves down, and cuffs tightly fastened. Sealed in that sort of (half) uniform. Always. Enrico is a lawyer, a colleague, a professional. But, as mentioned, he was also a key player in our gang. That's why sometimes, when we were with the same group, we would stay out until morning, after working late somewhere or maybe after a party. He would leave with me, strictly in a T-shirt or polo shirt, because he wasn't afraid of me, even though I was "his" CEO. We would leave together and together we covered the miles that separated us from the office. And then the same thing always happened. Stop at the highway service area, bathroom break, and the guy in the polo shirt would come out "armed" with a long-sleeve shirt. "I can't show up at work with these tattoos on..." Sure, maybe he could have been noticed by anyone, or even the CEO. Oh no... "Enrico, I'm here with you, we've known each other forever, I know your tattoos inside out, and you have to put on a shirt to go into the office?"

He did it because as soon as he got close to the workplace, as soon as he set foot inside, he felt he had to change. Getting out of a tunnel like that is no joke. Not because it's necessarily a serious thing, apart from the discomfort Enrico felt at the thought of being judged (or prejudged, to return to the subject of stereotypes). It was difficult because Enrico had entrusted his inviolable shirt with the task of safeguarding his peace of mind (no small thing for a shirt, after all). I tried hard to make him see reason, and after a while I managed to get him to let his guard down. But—and here lies the difficulty—when you leave your comfort zone, you are forced to experiment, at least until you find one that is the same or better. Thus began a period in which Enrico, having done away with "Mr. Hyde," became "Dr. Jekyll" 24 hours a day. Even too much so. But it was a brief interlude, because in the end he found a balance. He got there at a time in his life when he realized that at Var Group he could be who he was, in a long-sleeve shirt or polo, a T-shirt or suit. As long as he was truly happy and at ease.

Enrico is a case in point, perhaps the one closest to me, and therefore the one I can talk about most directly. But there have been many cases like this. Today, some time later, I must admit that I feel a certain sense of pride when I walk around the office and see people who have no difficulty being themselves, without filters, respecting the environment and the specific work they do. I mean, there is a certain amount of difficulty inherent in the very idea of work, which is useful and good and teaches us a lot.

But at the end of the day, when all is said and done, it's still work. Why add a gratuitous sense of oppression, why do you have to be someone else, or even feel resentful because you want to do something but aren't allowed to? What kind of cage does constantly keeping yourself in check create? And what damage does this do to people, to the company, and even to business?

Make work more fun

Happiness isn't everything. Neither is failure. Waging a war to the death against stereotypes, against pigeonholing in life or in organization charts, against the excessive rules that oppress us, isn't either. A workplace, a company, a group can be as free, agile, fast, and innovative as you want. It can be transparent, have ambition to spare, and put all of this "at the service of the market," as those in business say. But, believe it or not, all this can seriously remain a dead letter, stall, implode, or drown in a spiral of chaos if one thing above all else is not kept in mind. Which is always secondary to those who bring the company to life; those who populate it; those who carry it on their shoulders; those who make it grow, sweat over it, and strive for it. All of this is solely and exclusively at the service of people.

Be wary of those who sell people as "assets," as "human capital." Those who go out of their way to tell you how they "manage," forgetting to mention that problems are managed, while people are cared for. Those who think this way believe that it is enough to give orders. They do not know, and do not want to know, that the issue is something else entirely.

Leading for the sake of leading. Leading like you would lead a flock, head down and pedaling, and so what if you feel bad, don't understand, don't feel like yourself, and everything is falling apart. Stay away from these people, a thousand miles away. From what I have seen and experienced, from how I live it, the issue is quite different; the role you have to play, at most, is that of an enabler, a facilitator (full stop, almost nothing else is needed). Everything revolves around people, pe-ople. People are people, people like you and me. Those on the outside, the end customer, as well as those on the inside, the colleague. Families included, communities included.

To help Var Group move forward, to manage from within a process of evolution that was beginning to enter through the window, coming straight from the market, gliding and landing inside us, I looked to the people. In less uncertain times, I wanted to be a psychologist. Life had other plans, but some things take a long time to come full circle. I wanted to be a psychologist, and in the end, I somehow managed to become one.

Without people, without teams, you can't win the game. And they all have the same responsibility to help reach the finish line. Except that those who are used to giving orders risk sending "their" people to the slaughter, because by seeing them as assets or capital, they turn them into something impersonal, expendable pawns. And if they are expendable, when things go wrong, people are discarded, replaced, and that's that. The difference between those who empower and those who facilitate is enormous. It's another step forward, like the one Julio Velasco took when he moved from coaching the men's national volleyball team to the women's team. Playing with the same, identical people. First, he valued their differences, then he broke down stereotypes. In other words, he understood where, how, and when they could perform at their best, both for themselves and for the team. Ultimately, this meant bringing back into the game something that seemed lost, buried under a pile of disappointments, empty placings, and defeats.

That notable absence, that "uninvited guest," then as now, has a name: fun. Making work more fun, satisfying, and pleasant. Whether work involves playing volleyball or something else entirely. At Var Group, we focus on people; people win as a team, and teams "run smoothly" when they enjoy themselves.

Amici miei[1]

Having fun is something natural. We laugh to defuse tension, to relax, out of happiness or satisfaction, quite simply. It adds an extra touch of flavor to what we do. It's normal. But there are contexts in which all of this, however natural, tends to be repressed. Because tradition dictates that in those contexts, seriousness must reign at all costs. What utter nonsense to take oneself too seriously. For people with a "healthy madness" like us, it is absolutely unthinkable. Because we don't just have fun, we have a real culture of irreverence. This also involves a wide range of pranks. Now, when a group of courageous lunatics plan a prank, they don't limit themselves to a simple joke: they work on it, they use their ingenuity, they create. There is no room for the simple, the obvious, the predictable. The result is always something more, something artistic.

They put my house up for sale, choosing the most favorable time, when I was quite busy. I was getting a lot of phone calls. It was the end of the calendar year, just before Christmas, and even though that didn't coincide with the end of our fiscal year, we were still dealing with a flood of orders, coinciding with the closing of many clients' budgets. My phone rang frequently, often from numbers I didn't recognize, but so far, so good: I answered, listened, responded, and acted accordingly. The problem started when, between one "work" call and another, a series of other calls began, at first modest but then increasingly intrusive and disturbing: "Hello, I saw your house for sale on the web, I'm interested, if you could give me some more information, please..." "Look, I think you've got the wrong number, I'm sorry, but there's no other explanation..." I

---

[1] *Amici miei* (*My Friends*) is a 1975 Italian comedy film directed by Mario Monicelli.

said at first. After a while, it became just: "Wrong number." "Wrong number." "Wrong number." Always, constantly.

Until one day, like any other, with just a few extra decorations, I was at my desk when Mirko walked by. We had a meeting scheduled. As usual, my phone rang. But I changed the script: "Excuse me, may I ask why you keep calling me?" The guy on the other end just replied: "What do you mean? Are you Mrs. Monica?" "Look, I'm actually Francesca, not Monica..." "If you're not Mrs. Monica, I think the only explanation is that your cell phone number was mistakenly included in an ad for a penthouse for sale in Fucecchio." I asked her where the ad was. I went to the website. I found the ad. It wasn't bad at all. Obviously, it wasn't my house. They had created an ad with a series of photos, as is usually the case. Everything was normal, perfectly normal. Except that when specifying the contact details, whoever had created the ad had entered my work cell phone number. I turned to Mirko and drew what I thought was the most logical conclusion: "Mirko, damn it, she's got the wrong cell phone number, she's put mine!" Mirko, incidentally, is responsible for cybersecurity. Based on that single piece of information, my imagination ran wild: "What if I've been hacked? It's strange that they're calling me. The number, the house in Fucecchio, I live in Fucecchio... Could someone have stolen my credentials?" Mirko looked at me, thought about it for a moment, then said, "Try writing to her. Go to the ad site, find the message section, and try writing to the advertiser. Tell her, 'Look, the house is very popular, but unfortunately you put my number instead of yours, and I'm getting a ton of calls.'"

Amici miei – Atto II[2]

I took the bait. We went to lunch, then returned to our workstations. Then Mirko, from his desk, which at the time was on the other side of the office, sent me an email. It was the same one I had sent from the website. "Now what? So it's true, I've been hacked!" Nothing, I didn't get it. I didn't want to get it. Convinced that I was being held hostage by some cyber pirate, I rocketed off in Mirko's direction. As I ran, I noticed something. I felt like I was being watched, which was normal considering

---

[2] *Amici miei - Atto II* (*All My Friends* Part 2) is a 1982 Italian comedy film directed by Mario Monicelli, the sequel to 1975's Amici miei.

I run like a madwoman. But, on top of that, the people around me are laughing. What's so funny? I go over to Mirko and say, "See, I was right! You got her, though!"

Meanwhile, a crowd had gathered around us, made up of people who had been laughing while I was running and who had not only continued to laugh but had also followed me. "I got her, I got her," he reassured me, looking at me. Then there was a moment of silence as we stared at each other. "Don't you get it yet, Francesca? I'm the one who played a joke on you, who put your house up for sale..." That's why they were laughing. Because I was the only one who didn't know, who wasn't supposed to know, the only one was me.

To pull off a prank like that, it's not enough to be generally clever. It takes precise calculation of the dynamics, careful study of the victim and the methods, a lot of psychology, and the ability to strike where it hurts most, and when it hurts most. Prank is perhaps an understatement; it's an art form in its own right. Behind it all is "genius." And after all, "What is genius? It is imagination, intuition, decision, and speed of execution," to quote the stage, television and film actor Gastone Moschin.

Collective brains

I repeat: these are not just jokes for the sake of it. There is more to it than that. It is fun that is somehow serious. It is an intelligent diversion from normality, given the level of elaboration that we have achieved over time and with practice. It is also a socially unifying element, I would add. All this is what makes our work fun, and much more. It's a culture of fun, which comes across, for example, in a string of non-birthdays, when you send birthday wishes on Facebook in April to people who were actually born in December, so you can see them floundering as they respond to the many messages that follow, explaining that it's not true, that it's not their birthday, but thanks for thinking of them, and sending hugs and kisses. And then there are the phone calls, in addition to messages on social media, and in-person greetings at the office, etc. The flapping of a butterfly's wings that triggers an earthquake.

To orchestrate initiatives like these, however silly they may seem, you need a great mind. And since pranks are an aspect of our shared culture, we get stuck in and enjoy them to the fullest (it really is the case to say so).

They are a form of intelligence that is necessarily collective. Intelligence has no boundaries or homeland. Great ideas are born and can be born anywhere. In our case—and to quote one of my all-time favorite phrases—"the best ideas do not come from reason, but from a healthy and visionary madness." Yes, I wrote madness. Because this is also madness.

From my point of view, for the sake of absolute transparency and to remain faithful to the authentic version of events as I have recounted them so far, I have always had my best ideas during informal moments. Perhaps on evenings when we would sit down, strictly outside the office, and we were ourselves: a group of people, regardless of role, age, or seniority, and we would simply enjoy an entire evening talking, perhaps with an aperitif or a drink in front of us, snacks nearby, and music playing in the background. There, we would become like rivers in flood. We had the freedom to say whatever came to mind and to live our working lives authentically.

Improvised breeding grounds

The best initiatives of Var Group were born from improvised workshops like these. The first Kick Offs, conventions, even the first major organizational changes: the initial spark for all these things systematically came from here. When you sit around a table, whatever table it may be, and do nothing but feed the collective intelligence, from seven in the evening until three in the morning, talking without limits, without rules, without barriers, and about what you really want to talk about, at that exact moment you are not just passing the evening. The evening itself has nothing to do with it, quite the contrary. You are doing something much bigger and more meaningful. You are celebrating, perhaps. Celebrating an authentic moment that, as such, can make the night go one way or another. Celebrating the creativity that you can unleash because that's the place, wherever it is, and that's the moment, whatever time the clock says. I'm crazy about it. So much so that I've built a format around it, the *Var Talk*, where once every two months we bring together eighteen Var Group "leaders" to "institutionalize" that healthy madness in a magical regular event, where even the most daunting issues are seen in a whole new light, because we create the conditions to look at them from new angles.

Spaces like these and moments like these help us to step outside our comfort zone and our own space, enabling us to think in ways that are unfamiliar to us. Think of a pressure cooker filled with water. Put it on the stove and wait. The flame burns, the heat rises, the water boils and turns into steam. The steam is hot, it rises and pushes against the lid. But the pot is pressurized, and the lid is secured so it won't open. It keeps pushing, pushing, pushing, pushing. It pushes because, under those conditions, that's the only way it can react to the increasing heat, so the hotter it gets, the more the steam pushes. It pushes because the air expands, and the pot expands too, until everything blows up. Introduce a variation: add a valve. Now open the pot, let the steam out, and watch the pot return to its original size. The flame is still burning, the water is boiling, steam is being produced and rising, but this time it is free to escape. The freewheeling evenings of our group are the pressure release valve of our collective intelligence.

Chasing or predicting

Experience shows that the best ideas come up in fun, informal settings. Environments and contexts where the release valve works and does its job, giving you back the clarity you need to realize that things have many different angles, many shades, and that even the world, in its own right, is vaster and more multifaceted than you could have imagined from the safety of your own garden, however large or small. But that's not all, I would add. Because, in my opinion, inspiration and ideas are a bit like butterflies: they flit around and we need to be able to see them, to reach out at the right moment and catch them. To chase them, if necessary. Or to anticipate them, if needed.

I saw and experienced all this firsthand as Covid hit us. On March 6, 2020, all schools in Italy closed. It was too risky to remain open. At that time, Tuscany was, in a way, an oasis in the desert, because in that very early stage there were not yet enough cases to cause widespread alarm. One might have thought, then, that in that oasis and at that precise moment, closing schools in our region might be a bit excessive. For my part, I had already closed my offices in Milan and the Veneto region, and then in Bologna, where the restrictions were harsher than here. So I wasn't surprised that something was being done in our area too. That was my view, though. Because there were also people who didn't accept the closure at all; those who openly thought it was nonsense; those who didn't agree.

Meanwhile, on that very day, March 6, in the early afternoon, I was in my car, on my way to a business meeting in Florence. When I heard that schools were closing, the first thing that came to mind was to call Giovanni and tell him that, starting the next day, I would give anyone in Empoli who wanted to stay home the opportunity to do so as well. Because from that moment on, anyone with children would have a big problem, and I could say that because I was a mother of two, one in fifth grade and one in sixth grade. I made the call and the argument began. It grew and became furious. You don't want to rile up a former shouter, who is rebellious by DNA. Because even if she's on the road and has things to do, at the first opportunity she'll turn around and speed straight to the office. All the while screaming like an eagle. Because at 2:30 p.m. on a Wednesday afternoon, when schools have just closed, with Covid at the door and infections decimating half of Italy, you can't reasonably expect people to show up at the office at 9 a.m. the next morning, whistling and pretending nothing happened. It was unreasonable, it was impossible, and I wasn't going to stand for it.

So, back at the base and having informed the relevant people in Florence that the meeting was off, I prepared myself for a tough confrontation. And tough it was. Giovanni and Paolo chasing me down the corridors. Step after step after step. Shouting after me. Shouting at me. Shouting things. That I would ruin the company. That I didn't understand anything. That people don't work from home. Shouting, perhaps, doesn't quite convey the idea in that case. I kept going, resolute and with a lot of anger boiling inside me. Come hell or high water, the next day I would allow those who needed to stay at home to do so. I was told that people couldn't just stay at home like that, and that they would be automatically granted vacation time instead.

"Do your best, but according to how your family is organized"

Timing is an extraordinary thing. Even in a negative sense. Because they couldn't have made a worse proposal to me. Because it touched on a stereotype, one of the worst in my opinion, that of gender. 99 times out of

100, who is going to stay at home? Women, of course; who in that period unfortunately made giant strides, but backwards, because the first reaction, the most "comfortable" one, is that in an emergency situation like this, it is the woman who stays home. I thought and thought. I thought about the Empoli headquarters, where there were offices with only women or almost entirely populated by women, such as the back office. How could we tell all of them, who were mothers and therefore would have their children at home right away: "So, tomorrow at 9 a.m. you have to be at work; if you can't, take vacation time"? With what kind of nerve, and on what grounds?

Beyond the act itself, something like this would not save a company (and this was the concern on the other side); it would shut it down immediately. In the end, we went to the back office; I went to them. "Do your best, but according to how your family is organized" was the only thing I felt I could say. That colossal, colorful, bombastic argument opened a Pandora's box. If possible—as is my habit whenever I find myself facing a closed door—it convinced me to press on. I did exactly as I saw fit. I responded first to common sense and the urgency of caring for people rather than to dictates.

There was a lot of chatter about Hamlet-like dilemmas, such as "Everyone is at home, what do we do now?" and similar comments. For me, it was background noise. Like the blah blah blah they put in comic strips to show that something is being said, but the something, at that moment in the story, doesn't really carry much weight. It was blah blah blah and nothing more to me, because I had already taken my own precautions, unbeknownst to everyone except my own common sense. Two weeks before the end, I had instructed team leaders throughout Italy, but particularly in Empoli, to get organized because the risk of a total lockdown was very high. We had made an emergency plan for the data center after I had studied everything I could find about what had already happened in China, where rules had been issued preventing access precisely to data centers. We had our "disaster case," we knew what to do even if at some point we were denied access. I had organized everything so that we could leave people at home as calmly as possible, while still allowing them to continue working. Laptops, cell phones, connectivity; for the entire Var Group population. An entire company leaving the office and taking their work home.

Three days later

Three days later, they closed everything down. We were at home. And Giovanni insisted that I would ruin the company. We held on as best we could, and even better than that. Apart from the first two or three weeks, when I couldn't sleep because I felt a responsibility as heavy as the two thousand people who worked with us at the time. Those were tough weeks, with one eye trained on the stock market, which was floundering. It was a constant alert, but what wasn't, and where, in the midst of Covid?

There were some temporary unemployment benefits available, because the government had made this available for the commercial sector. I had thought it through beforehand and set up a series of video calls with all the teams, one by one, until I reached two thousand people. Temporary unemployment was used to cover one day of absence, and the typical week became: one day vacation time, one day unemployment, and three days working from home. In the video calls, I wanted to explain why we were activating the unemployment option. That I couldn't know exactly what would happen, and that we were necessarily playing it a bit by ear. That it would be a kind of marathon. And that in that marathon and in that perhaps prolonged uncertainty, given that we were being offered a breath of fresh air, it was right to take the opportunity. The company fronted the benefits. We prepaid them so that people would not suffer any financial hardship; this is and remains a point of honor for me.

We gritted our teeth and made sacrifices. And then, at a certain point, it happened. Everything took off again. Partly because our sector experienced tremendous growth thanks to Covid. Partly because, like brave and mad people, we decided to persevere and be stronger than a fate that reduced us to a minimum. Partly because we were able to organize ourselves, despite everything, to become as close as possible to what the market demanded. The market demanded technological remote working: we were technological remote working. Whatever the main reason, and whatever the secondary ones, at the end of the 2020 fiscal year, we achieved great results; the best ever, in fact.

In the midst of that crazy storm, we had suspended bonuses. We reinstated them, with an increase due precisely to the excellent results we managed to achieve. Those bonuses were of the people, and for the people. For their families and for the whole community around us. For them, for us, for the entire Var Group it was a huge sacrifice, an enormous sacrifice. Because, apart from temporary unemployment and vacation time, people worked five days a week from home. They had to work because they didn't know what else to do to keep themselves busy, or at least to train themselves, and they had to push even harder because their work was needed more than ever at that precise moment. A huge effort was required, and a huge effort was achieved. Now it was time to reap the rewards for all this.

Other rewards

Beyond the financial results that came out of that superhuman marathon (but also the moral and social responsibility for families and the community as a whole), Covid brought us at least a couple of other rewards. The first was that we got a taste for remote working. For me, who was already accustomed to self-directed experiments before they became mainstream, since the days of Computer Gross, the fact that people were talking openly about smart working and then starting to implement it in a structured way seemed like connecting the dots, the official crowning glory of something I had invested in myself, in less suspicious times, taking all the necessary criticism, just because I wanted to look where others stubbornly turned their backs.

At the time, I had begun to lift the veil, but the time was not yet ripe to take a clear stance and assert myself. So, my first attempts at smart working were more like secret initiatives, with the constant pressure of being opposed and having to deal with the usual accusation: if you allow this, you are allowing the company to go under. In truth, time is a great leveler, and in the end, it was only the clumsy obsessions of those who pointed the finger at me that went down the drain.

Today, we all have individual contracts. For everyone, with everyone's full approval, it is established in writing, in black and white, that every week there are two days of remote work on average. Depending on the circumstances and requirements, this may be less or more. It seems like the least we can do, and as a result, I know that I will soon be back to putting my mind to it, in a company that considers itself unique and bold, but also disciplined and consistent. A company that strives to be fluid and, with its IT skills, makes it a duty to help businesses on their journey of digital transformation.

And then there is the other gift of the post-pandemic era: the redesign of work environments, as a direct consequence of the change in the way we work, which Covid has accelerated significantly. This was significant for me in particular, mind you, because before the lockdown, I always had an almost automatic preference for physical presence when it came to meetings. Programs like Teams were out of the question. To be honest, I had a device on my desk that would have been well suited to the purpose, but I used it sporadically and awkwardly.

A result of Covid, a consequence of smart working

Upon closer inspection, the redesign of spaces was not only a result of Covid, but also a direct consequence of the smart working model we adopted, first full-time and then on a more flexible basis. If you do a lot of remote work, if you can easily manage meetings just as effectively, if not more so, in front of a screen, what is the point of having huge spaces? Large rooms with too many desks (and very few meeting rooms): what exactly are we supposed to do with them? The issue was not so simple, nor was it automatic, in truth. Because we already had the space; we had built it, we hadn't inherited it. So it was impossible to think of giving that space up or selling it to move – and then, in a world that is moving in a new direction, who would ever consider it?

It wasn't easy, and after a series of internal discussions, we realized that to find the real and decisive key to the puzzle, we had to look not only inward, but also outward. We found a consulting firm specializing in redesigning work environments based on organizational changes. People we could count on because their design of the offices would be part of a larger overall design, that of the evolving organization. As the organization evolved, we wanted the work environment to accompany that development.

The consulting firm, which specializes in design thinking and is called Lombardini 22, came in, did its thinking, and then developed an *ad hoc* survey, which it launched among the entire workforce of the two most important offices that were about to open at that exact moment: Milan and Bologna. They did a "complete overhaul," asking people questions ranging from the practical to the theoretical, from what they considered appropriate and necessary in a workspace to what values they would like to find in the office. The consultants collected the results, organized them, and we sifted through them; inch by inch.

With the results at the center, we transformed them into a careful process of reformulating and redesigning the work environments. In doing so, I confess that my earliest memories of landing at Var Group often came to mind. This was partly due to natural sentimentality, because I was witnessing and actively participating in the end of an era that was part of my own memories, albeit relatively recent ones. Partly, however, it was out of contrast. Because in my head and in my gut, I knew that we were moving towards something else. That Var Group was on its way to achieving a goal, an open organization, in which it simply made no sense, for example, to keep individual offices. So away with all the individual offices. For calls, we needed not just a few but many rooms, of various sizes, perhaps with medium-sized ones for small meetings or group work, and larger ones for structured meetings or meetings with many participants. And then, lounges and shared spaces scattered throughout each area. And by popular demand, lots and lots of plants. Because one of the most important values that everyone had indicated was green. In a burst of initiative, I fully supported that legitimate request and made it my own, and I had insisted that the offices in Milan, Bologna, Treviso, Turin, and Rome all have this common thread. Huge flower boxes and bookcases with small bags containing small plants.

Giovanni was also there while we were "messing around" with these things. He was there, and at one point he fired his wisely considered question at me: "But are you hiring a gardener? How are you going to manage all these plants?" I didn't want to listen to him and thus I set myself up for another resounding defeat. Because he was absolutely right. Between Milan, Bologna, Treviso, Turin, and Rome, we had adopted the Amazon rainforest. And there was no one who was seriously willing to take care of it. You can't give people greenery and then let it die in front of them. Then came the lightbulb moment. Which, in my opinion, still represents one of the pinnacles of human ingenuity. There are companies that offer green-as-a-service: they rent plants, working throughout Italy, including planting, maintenance, and care. They come, check, water, prune, treat, and if one dies, they replace it immediately. Done. Contract negotiated in all locations, absolutely reasonable rate. Game, set, match.

The Round Table, according to us

The image of this redesign, even with all its Amazonian marvels, would not be complete without mentioning the "highlight." By physically removing traditional offices, and with them every socially segregated area, we couldn't help but set a good example. And we couldn't help but do it in our own crazy way. All offices have lost their individual rooms. Among the individual offices, the first to disappear were obviously the managerial ones. Today, we have managers who sit together and work in an open-plan office. They can do this, and they do, because we have created a series of Leadership Tables. These are round tables, not in the geometric sense but more in the epic sense, where people share the same space, sit next to each other and (after defeating a bit of resistance to change, which I managed to overcome in real time, you can enjoy a job where everything is more immediate, easier, more shareable, and transparent.

The Leadership Table ended up changing us deeply. In the sense that it made us more of a team, breaking down the time it used to take us to get on the same page, pushing us to be more open about ourselves, to get to know each other and bond more than we were able to in the past. The effect has been miraculous and total, in the sense that it has given us greater satisfaction, and has affected not only those who always play the role of "early adopters," demonstrating greater responsiveness and proactivity towards anything new, but the whole team.

Fabio is a great guy; he grew up with Giovanni and sits right next to me. But when he works, he likes to wear headphones because it helps him concentrate. I'm really glad he's focused, but before, I had a hard time connecting with him. What's more, by nature, if he wasn't given direction, he tended to do lots of things at once, risking losing track of things along the way. It wasn't a big deal, he just needed more interaction. More interaction, or a nice place at the Leadership Table, where it only takes a moment to talk to each other, to understand where we are and what we need to do in coordination. So now, if I want to talk to Fabio, all I have to do is wait for him to take off his headphones to go to the bathroom and corner him (maybe when he comes back, so he's even more relieved). The advantage, moreover, is not only mine: since Fabio is someone who is always afraid of disturbing others, in such a context and through immediate contact, he loses that little bit of shyness and goes on more peacefully.

Good stories and innovation

Good stories are wonderful, but they all have one limitation: they are closed boxes. Sealed. Packaged. Hermetic. Done and dusted. New ideas, innovation, and evolution, by their very nature, do not have these characteristics: above all, they never have a happy ending, and not because they are sad; they don't have one because they have no end. There is always something to improve, perfect, develop, transform and evolve further, for the better. Can you imagine a fairy tale that never ends, because after the prince saves the princess (or after the princess saves herself), something more, something better, something bigger always has to be added? *That's the difference.*

I wouldn't be totally honest and transparent with you, who are taking the trouble to read and pay attention to me, if I told you that we've reached the finish line, that everything is running smoothly, that we're at the top of our game; that nothing could be better, grow further, or be perfected. The redesign is no exception.

With the advent of smart working, workstations in our offices have become strictly free, unassigned, and left to individual initiative. Theoretically, those who arrive in the morning could choose the first seat they see, then rotate according to their preferences and schedule. Everything is in perfect condition for rotation. Theoretically. Because in fact, habit is what psychologically speaking contributes to making us human. And eradicating a habit is one of the most difficult processes to achieve. There are too many family photos, gadgets, and various knick-knacks on desks not to still feel that these are someone's favorite places and, as such, the places they habitually use. Even if the person who usually uses them is not there at that moment and may not return until the next day or the day after that. The issue arises when someone arrives at the office and cannot find a place to sit down; they cannot find one because, faced with spaces that have already been colonized, they always feel like they are appropriating a place that is somehow occupied.

My current battle—one of my battles, to be more precise—is against those who deliberately leave personal items at their workstations, leaving them there even when they go, and expecting to find "their" place "reserved" for them. I have often been tempted to take everything and throw it out of the window. To go from desk to desk, remove personal belongings and see how they fare flying from a medium-high floor. But I am a former shouter, a former Computer Gross beast, an iconoclast and a rebel. I want to leverage the power of persuasion. I will try and try again, searching for the best way to make myself understood. In the meantime, even though it is difficult, I record everything in my notebook under the heading "areas for improvement in the future."

The big NO

No to hierarchies, yes to roles and responsibilities.

No to formalism, yes to collective intelligence, especially in informal contexts.

No to exhausting and meaningless work, yes to healthy effort, the kind that is good for us, for the company, and for everything around us, our families, the community, and the "world."

No to taking ourselves too seriously, yes to having fun, enjoying ourselves while working and working while enjoying ourselves.

Growing up and making my way, I had collected many "nos," which had arisen within me, which I had tried to systematize in order to break down things that didn't work, that could not go on, things that always had sharp claws and hurt continuously. To break them down, dismantle them, and replace them with as many "yeses" that, from what I felt and saw, could bring with them the promise of something more and better.

However, the list, and above all the assessment, would not be complete if I glossed over the "no" that has perhaps accompanied me for the longest time. A capital NO, dense and primordial for me. The first one I had to deal with. Public enemy number one. The no that I have always wanted to oppose to stereotyping. Which for me has meant, and still means, a number of things: being a woman in this world. Removing myself from social conditioning. Embarking on the daily struggle for freedom from the bonds of a subtle phenomenon that has a name that inspires horror and fear (but more horror): it's called gender servitude.

As soon as I joined Computer Gross, the first job I was given was a task that did not just challenge my level of tolerance, but went beyond it. Having duly noted this, after banging my fists on the table to make myself clear, leaving no room for doubt, and seriously threatening to leave, what I got was a job as Credit Manager. Credit Manager meant exactly what it said: I was responsible for a team. And so far, so good. However, there was Alessandro in the team, someone who had been working at Computer Gross for a thousand years, young but born and raised in that company (and who, incidentally, took my place after I joined Var Group, becoming Credit Manager himself). The responsibility for that team, including Alessandro, was the only thing that was truly certain at the time. Because that figure, the Credit Manager, did not actually exist before. Until then, that working group had naturally gathered around the most experienced people who worked there and who, in practice, acted as Credit Managers and had a certain reputation for that role, but without any official appointment. Alessandro was in exactly that position: they knew him and recognized him as that figure, even though he didn't actually do that job but something else. For my part, I was only twenty-seven, so age didn't really work in my favor in terms of experience.

"Can you bring us some coffee?"

When work took Alessandro and me to visit retailers (our clientele at the time), the same thing always happened. Namely, I was the one who was asked, as politely as possible, to bring the coffee. I was automatically identified as the assistant. No one, and I mean no one, even considered that I could be the Credit Manager and that he was a member of "my" team. I would look up, swallow that bitter pill, but in the end, I would always bury the hatchet. After all, I was only twenty-seven and had just arrived, while Alessandro had a well-established reputation.

The problem, aside from my ability to put up with it, arose when I began to realize that it was continuing. Even as I grew older and more senior, episodes like this continued to take place, regularly. The point was not that of the young woman against the senior, the newcomer against the established figure. Behind and within there was much more: an unconscious machismo that is rooted in our brains, where by "our" I mean both men's and women's.

One evening, while traveling in Rome, I decided to organize a dinner at a Michelin-starred restaurant with a magnificent view and a renowned chef in charge of the kitchen. I made the arrangements, booked the table, and invited my four guests, who, in honor of such a formal occasion, all showed up wearing ties. We sat down, enjoyed the refined atmosphere for a while, and shortly afterwards a waiter approached us with the menus. The menus were neatly distributed, and we began to consult them to choose our dishes. These were menus from a Michelin-starred restaurant, with many courses and options, and each dish took up a generous line just for its name. Yet, even in this riot of names and courses, something was missing. I noticed it immediately, but the others didn't. They didn't, because everything was fine on their menus. On mine, however, there were no prices. No prices for the appetizers. Nothing for the first courses. Nothing for the second courses, side dishes, or desserts. Not even for the cover charge. Only my menu was like this. A mistake by the restaurant, which perhaps inadvertently left an old version in the pile, or maybe a print sample? My fellow diners didn't know what to say to me. This had never happened to them. The only thing to do was to point it out to the waiter. He was called, arrived in a flash, and revealed the "mystery." My menu was correct. It will always be like this. Because it is customary for women not to see the prices. Custom, tradition, chivalry, delicacy.

Meal or gift?

The fact is—and this was the waiter speaking, in response to my specific question about why this "custom" exists—that when you invite someone to lunch or dinner, you are not simply offering them a meal, but giving them a gift. And when you give a gift, since the dawn of time, everything is said except how much was spent. A menu without prices is the equivalent of a courtesy receipt. A kindness, in fact. But a kindness is only such if it is not contaminated by anything else. In this specific case (but there are many others), by a culturally and intrinsically patriarchal society. Who decided that because I was a woman, I should be offered dinner? Who made it automatic that the man pays and the woman does not? Who debased something that started out as a kind gesture (offering the recipient of a gift, whoever they may be, a menu without prices) and turned it into something completely different?

These are surely the same people who came up with the "golden rule" that waiters should serve women first. Perhaps they are oblivious to the fact that at a business dinner for people who work in a sector such as mine (I say this not by chance, but from direct experience), out of a total of twenty people, there are maybe three women, scattered among the crowd and perhaps sitting in the corners that are hardest to reach. And so the waiter takes the dish from the kitchen, brings it to the dining room, and then makes a whole procession with trajectories that even a ballistics expert would struggle to understand... all to serve the women first, always the women first. Why? What's the point? Is this still etiquette or have we sunk into arbitrariness? And if only it were confined to the table—still serious, but at least limited...

I go from one meeting to another for work. That's part of my job. But sometimes, more often than you can imagine, I have to deal with male counterparts. And they do nothing but talk, addressing not me, but my colleague sitting next to me. Who is also a man, "obviously," because as you can guess from the previous example, ours is a world made up of men, so nine times out of ten, the person sitting next to me in a meeting is a man. I don't think it's male solidarity, and I don't even believe in male solidarity per se (nor, incidentally, in female solidarity). I believe we have big and urgent problems, and I believe we have them together, men and women.

"Ladies first..."

Another face-to-face meeting. With an important, high-ranking contact, as they say. All the more reason for me to keep my mouth shut. He arrives, I greet him, we shake hands, and I lead him to the room where we are to meet. The door is open, and he immediately starts off on the wrong foot—shortly after, it gets worse, I might add. We are about to enter the room, I step aside, extend my arm in the classic gesture followed by a simple "Please," inviting him to enter and take his seat. He stops, looks at me and replies, "No, no, ladies first..." I jump, but not enough to show it. Why? Because if we're "at my house," let me lead you, let me accompany you, and you go in first! How rude would I be to go in first? You're the guest, you go in first because that's a space I want to offer you at that moment, and I want you to be comfortable, to arrive and choose the seat you prefer.

It starts badly, but continues even worse, I said. Because at a certain point we decide to take the classic coffee break. We get up, line up to leave, and here too... ladies first. I tremble. We manage to leave the room and head for the break area. He lets slip a swear word. I don't bat an eyelid. But he feels compelled to smooth things over by adding, "I apologize to the ladies..." I stare at him and glare at him: "Maybe you should apologize to him [my colleague] who isn't familiar with this, I say more such words than you..." I try to smile, but a sarcastic expression slips out. Back in the meeting, he comments as expected; he talks and looks at the sales rep next to me, leaning towards him: he talks only to him. Let's end this sad story here, you might say.

But no. We end up talking about patriarchy. And the host feels compelled to reassure us: "I don't have a problem with 'this women thing'... I have three daughters myself." You do have a problem, because you reduce all of this to "this women thing." And you have an even bigger problem because you feel good about yourself since you have daughters. But your problems, my friend, are nothing compared to what those three daughters will face, especially if you don't decide to open your eyes first.

Episodes like these are a constant. And the bad thing about a constant is that, in its own way, it is absolutely "democratic." In the sense that it becomes a matter of stereotypes that afflict men as much as women.

"Mr. Notary"

The story of the notary is there to remind me of this. Some time ago, I happened to be present at a notarial deed. Opposite me, as the "counterparty" to the agreement, was a company that was joining the Group and had recommended this notary, whom I did not know. We met online and, after the usual pleasantries, the notary – a woman—began reading the draft deed. Being online, and so as not to disturb the reading with various noises, I muted the sound. She recited the first few lines, the heading of the deed, which also mentioned me ("Mrs. Francesca Moriani..."), then she stopped and asked me, "Excuse me, are you Ms. or Dr.?" I unmuted myself: "If you're asking me, I'm Dr., but it doesn't matter, I'm not offended." And I muted myself again.

She continued reading the deed. Among those present was also the statutory auditor. He was also mentioned in the reading. But as Dr. So-and-so. Without stopping, without asking if he was a doctor or a gentleman. They needed to verify my identity, but not his. I notice this, and I'm not the only one. He takes off his headphones, stops the notary and says, "No, look, I'm not a 'doctor,' please write 'Mr.' because I don't have a degree." He wasn't a doctor, but he was still a great man. For me, above all, it was hope. Hope that not only will people begin to notice distortions like this, which always pull in one direction and always to the detriment of one side, but that something will be done about it. That men will do something about it. And that women will too. Including the woman who was "Mr. Notary" in this case, who still had a long way to go before she became fully aware of this.

Beforehand, there was a wall of silence. But now, little by little, something is starting to move. Something is slowly changing. You notice it from the number of people—men and women—who are beginning to notice that something is wrong, very wrong. That enough is enough. That another way and another world are possible. You notice it in the little things. The things that surround you and happen right next to you.

My current partner Alex (no weddings, add him to the list) is a martyr in this regard, just like Diego and Cesare (but if we were talking about my mother, it would be exactly the same story, believe me). All three of them have me in common, in that I've been nagging them about this practically forever (it's no coincidence that this year I was awarded the Microsoft Power Women Award Italy, but in total absentia, since the nomination was made and sent under the table by my colleagues). Well, just a few days ago, Alex sent me a photograph taken while he was watching his niece's synchronized swimming competition. The photo showed the female coach, whose shirt bore the word "Coach," written in the masculine version in Italian. He had seen it, taken the photo without thinking twice, and sent it to me, commenting that he was now starting to notice things like that. Not only that, he had also asked his daughter, sitting next to him and with the same view, if she saw anything strange around her. Unfortunately, she just shook her head. Everything was normal. In that exchange on the steps of a swimming pool like so many others, there is what we should aspire to in order to change things, on the one hand, and what risks happening if we continue to look the other way, on the other.

Awareness is needed. A lot of it. Right now. We need a vague awareness to break down a habit that has lasted for millennia. To ensure that what I consider the most difficult day of the year, March 8 – International Women's Day – stops being a mere occasion to cover ourselves in mimosas and Baci Perugina chocolates, and becomes something more. More consistent with its original meaning: a day to remember not only the rights that women have had to fight so hard for, but also the social, political, and economic achievements that have brought us to where we are today. And less offensive than the low-brow, commercial, and contaminated recycling of what is certainly not a "celebration," but a day of reflection. To become aware and start looking around us properly. To kick out a few more stereotypes. No gender servitude, no more.

"Epilogue" (Kick Off)

The modern fruit of an ancient *joie de vivre*

May in Florence is an extraordinary month, when you can afford the luxury of losing yourself under a warm sun, with the scent of azaleas, peonies, and roses filling the air, rising directly from the gardens scattered within the city walls. It couldn't be otherwise in a city known as the "city of the flower." And then there is *Maggio Musicale* (Florence Musical May). An institution for the city, with a long history dating back to the 1930s. Heir to a tradition of musical festivals, the *maggiolate*, which—leading with the seasonal celebration *Maypole*—stole *that* very month to celebrate the luxuriance of spring. A modern fruit of that ancient *joie de vivre* sung by Angelo Poliziano and Lorenzo il Magnifico, which marks the cyclical rebirth of a city bathed in flowers.

The Florence Musical May: operas and concerts, ballets and prose. From the Boboli Gardens to the Pergola Theater, from Piazza della Signoria to the Comunale, where it had found a permanent home. Then, with the new millennium just around the corner and the season of large metropolitan auditoriums, the "old" Comunale was replaced by a modern complex. Built in the same place, just a stone's throw from the Parco delle Cascine (Cascine Park) and the Porta al Prato station (Meadow Gate), the new home of the Maggio Musicale boasts 1,890 seats in the opera hall, 1,200 in the hall for symphony concerts and chamber music (this hall bears the name of maestro Zubin Mehta), plus an open-air auditorium that adds another 2,000 seats. A "city" of over five thousand seats, squeezed into a structure that, when dressed up (and with the right light, that of twilight), is reminiscent of the grandeur of a Egyptian temple;

and, on either side, it pierces the uneven ground on which it stands with stairways pointing to the clouds, worthy of a Mesoamerican pyramid.

For us at Var Group, in 2024, on the 28th of a month that could only be May, that "city" of seats halfway between Luxor and the Yucatan was even more than that, if possible: the much-desired venue for a new Kick Off. Nine years and a few months after the episode with which I opened this story, now quite a few pages ago: the tradition of the most classic of "big events" to kick off the new year.

An easy year

From 2015 to today, and from the Principe di Piemonte in Viareggio to the Maggio Fiorentino, countless things have changed. For me, for my life, for my work, for Var Group, for its entire population. Kick Off 2024 seen "through Francesca's eyes" was—first and foremost, and from the heart—an event to approach lightly. It was easy, but it was by no means a foregone conclusion. It was easy because so many things were thought out, organized, done, and finished without my direct involvement. Because the organizational machine worked like in my best dreams, where I walk around the company and things happen by themselves, where things happen and I don't even have to know about them because, quite simply, everything is fine.

The three hundred people who crowded into the hall in Viareggio became eighteen hundred. Six times as many. So many, in fact, that they filled a space normally used for opera performances. So many, but not enough, not yet at least, given that our company population, at the time of writing, stands at 3,850, and I am left with only one regret: that of not having had them all there, one by one.

There was a time when organizing a Kick Off was a risky business. The more effort you put into it, the harder it was. It was difficult to find things, themes, topics, and perspectives that could really interest everyone present. Especially in a company that, according to the figures, was growing and expanding, gaining an increasing share of diversity. So finding cross-cutting, "all-season" items that would work universally was a really tough challenge.

But 2024, on the Kick Off side, was a year of change, and for the better. An easy year, in fact, in which everything fell into place. One of those years in which many things that previously created mass and confusion ended up thinning out and disappearing on their own, with the veil tearing and lifting, revealing something clear that you recognize without hesitation at first glance. Because it is precisely what you are aiming for, what you are all aiming for. And so, as if by magic, you let it flow and find yourself holding something that makes sense, that really makes sense to tell, because it speaks of a shared heritage and, as such, has the gift of resonating with every individual.

Stop and celebrate

My first Kick Off, back in 2015, was also a break with tradition in its own way. Because when I got involved, I deliberately chose to break with tradition. The tradition of order that, until then, had marked an event limited in time, consisting of work, work, work, with a final "consolation" lunch at the end of which, invariably, everyone packed up and headed home. Year after year, inch by inch, that *démodée* tradition that I relentlessly chipped away at was replaced by a different certainty. Better still: one that was exactly the opposite.

The wise man says: "If you realize you've arrived somewhere, stop, and celebrate." The extremely busy period that began to falter in 2015 under the blows of a loudmouth like myself has changed over time. It has become a time to celebrate. A time when we come together not out of duty, but for the pleasure of meeting each other, and with that same pleasure we celebrate together. A time that undoubtedly also includes a session, the plenary, where we do something similar to work.

But we do it with grace and extreme delicacy. Two hours or so. Almost as if to pass the time before diving into the whirlwind of the cocktail, the dinner, the DJ set, and everything else that an evening like this has in store for us. With grace and delicacy, I repeat. Because those two hours are meant to be something else. Light. Fun. And, above all, inspiring. Stuff that doesn't leave you indifferent, that can't leave you unmoved. Stuff that stays with you once the event is over. That follows you home and back to the office. That keeps you company. And that stimulates you and gives you food for thought from then on.

May 28, 2024

The room is pitch black. The animated graphics start on the screen, pulsing to the beat of the music and projecting a countdown. When the countdown reaches zero, on the screen "Out Of Office" appears, half white and half purple, with the O's in the column resembling the helices of DNA, and a payoff that reads: "Enjoy the crew." It's May 28, and we're out of the office, on a day that is undisturbed and ours alone.

The next shot shows Ylenia in the center, who has been with Var Group for just a few months. It's her first Kick Off, and she's as tense as a violin string. She's totally nervous, just like I was in 2015. Absolutely perfect for introducing herself and calling me up on stage. I go up, we exchange a few words, and she passes the ball to me. I don't like beating around the bush; least of all in a Kick Off like this. The swing tune starts and I get straight to the point. Which, in this case, is numbers.

Turnover in 2024: € 815 million. EBITDA: € 100 million. 3,800 employees in Italy and 12 other countries. A virtual hug, speaking of people, to all those who, like Ylenia, are experiencing their first Kick Off and to those following online. My best wishes to the entire Var Group population, because results like these cannot be achieved by individuals, but only together.

Outlook for 2025: I recall the purpose of Var Group, which was founded and exists to accompany companies on their journey of digital transformation. With a clear and ambitious goal: to contribute to the economic and social well-being of the country by bringing innovative solutions to the market, society, and the ecosystem. And I ask the first question. Just like that. "In your opinion, are we doing this?" I go even further: "Above all, are we doing it as well as we should be?"

In my opinion – and I would like to share this impression – we are doing it, but only partially. Because such a goal cannot be achieved overnight. Something fundamental is needed. A new organizational model. A new corporate culture capable of adapting quickly, flexibly, and dynamically to changes in the economy, the market, and society. Changes that have become faster and more sudden than ever before.

"I am Var Group"

We need a new organizational model based on collaboration, sharing, and shared knowledge. On the desire to learn, study, and understand. To scratch the surface. We need a new model that values people and skills. That values us, first and foremost, as individuals, each one unique and irreplaceable. A model that recognizes diversity not as something to be feared but as an enormous source of wealth. That encourages listening, dialogue, and understanding, a culture of feedback and reflection.

Beautiful, wonderful. And it's been talked about for a while now at Var Group. Open organizations, distributed leadership. But the point is: how can we make it happen, starting from our daily routine? How can we contribute concretely to a model that focuses entirely on people's well-being and market satisfaction?

The answer: training and practice. So, our 2025 will be: training and practice. Training that people must believe in. Practice to be done together. With a commitment to give it our all, to reach every single individual. Because our entire community, myself included, needs to acquire new skills. Tools that enable us to make things happen in our daily lives. But we need to know how, and we need to invest in people's culture, in processes, and in platforms. 2025 will be the year of concentrated investment in these areas. Because only when we are convinced that what we see as a challenge is also the right path, only then can we proudly say: "I am Var Group. I contribute to these results with my daily work." It takes courage and tenacity, discipline and audacity. Without them, we would continue to stand still, doing what we have always done. A foolish luxury that we can no longer afford. We must look beyond, do new things. For the common good. We can become a company where people feel good and live well. And say with pride: *"I am Var Group."*

The split

Not another word. Seven and a half minutes, the time it takes to cover five hundred meters at a brisk pace. Seven and a half minutes, because I don't like beating around the bush. Least of all in a Kick Off like this. I speak, and I only think about speaking clearly. It would never have occurred to me that, in those five hundred meters of chatter, I wasn't actually just talking. That once I was done, there would be those who would come up to me to tell me, in no uncertain terms, that mine had not been a "simple" speech, but "the" speech, the one about organizational change. Because, in the broader view, and unconsciously for me, no one had ever seen me go so straight to what needed to be done. Precise, direct, without smudges.

Meanwhile, on that May 28, I don't know all this "background," I just want to speak clearly, and in a moment my speech is good and finished. The Kick Off, however, continues with Priel Korenfeld of Kopernicana.

"Organizing humans, humanizing organizations"

Priel has an extraordinary ability to inspire. He inspires because he is the first to be inspired, and you understand this immediately when you exchange a few words with him. What's more, he fully understands the evolutionary process I touched on in my speech. He is as involved as I am in the change of pace I dream of for Var Group. He is an organizational hacker, someone who—to borrow his motto—organizes humans with one hand and humanizes organizations with the other. He is a hacker because he is passionate about a technique. He is a hacker because that same passion has "enabled" him to get involved. To change what is wrong and needs to be changed. To improve it and then share the results.

Priel is someone who connects things and people. In Florence in particular, following a common thread that began with the previous Kick Off event, which Kopernicana (of which Priel is a partner) also attended, he connects his personal story with the adventure we are experiencing together, which speaks precisely to the organizational model of the Var Group to come. He says that all organizations are always grappling with a huge problem: trying to balance the autonomy of the parts, on the one hand, with their coherence on the other. Autonomy because everyone must be able to do their job without constantly getting stuck, so that the organization runs smoothly and the machine works. Coherence because all parts must move in the same direction, follow the same strategy, and achieve the same goals. Too much coherence, and the gears jam. Too much autonomy, and the common momentum is lost.

To resolve all this, hierarchical organizations always resort to the same answer: *command & control*. A culture of prohibition. Literally: you can't do anything unless you are told exactly what to do. This is usually how we grow up. Both at school and in our first jobs, we cultivate a sacred fear of doing and making mistakes. Because mistakes are costly. And so, rather than acting, we prefer to wait and see what room we have. However, in doing so, we build (and contribute to) slow, rigid organizations that are anything but flexible, and uninhabitable for people. This cannot be the future, and on closer inspection, not even the present. There must be another way.

Rare birds

Indeed, there is. And it comes from the many new ways of working that companies of all shapes, sizes, and industries have been actively experimenting with for decades. At first, they were few and far between, but now there are many examples. And the more time passes, the more they multiply. There are those who hold meetings where everyone really has the opportunity to contribute, where decisions are actually made; and when you leave, you do so with greater energy. There are companies where the roles that determine what I can expect from you and what you can expect from me are defined in detail and are transparent throughout the organization. These roles can be changed if necessary, with decisions being made together.

When you talk about these models, they sound like fairy tales, perhaps. In reality, they are concrete, real. They happen and run their course in companies that are adaptive and "welcoming" towards people. When you talk about them, they sound like some kind of upheaval or revolution. In reality, they are simply the result of intelligent common sense, based on a specific fact: when you think about it, outside of work we are independent, we can choose to take the car, take the route we like best, go where we want to go—provided we have a driver's license, obey the rules of the road, or at least not get caught committing serious offenses. In everyday life, there is no place for the culture of prohibition. It is a world where a different kind of system prevails, one that is totally different and opposite: the culture of permission. In everyday life, you can do whatever you want, unless there is a shared rule that says you can't do something, thus limiting our freedom to decide to do it.

So why, if the world is turning in one direction, is life in companies going in exactly the opposite direction? Because we are the ones making it go that way! Because that is usually the direction education takes. And because, as a result, it becomes habitual and familiar to us for things to go in exactly this way. So everything stays in its place. It is our responsibility. Just as it is our responsibility to free ourselves from it.

Hopper

Grace Hopper was a mathematician and computer scientist, one of the first in the world. She invented the COBOL language, and she was also a soldier in the United States Army. Grace Hopper said, "It's better to ask for forgiveness than permission." In other words, it's better to try something that goes beyond the limits, beyond the territory where we know everything works well. It's better to give, go further, and then, if necessary, fix things. Better than asking for permission.

The combination of apology/permission contains all of the difference between those who decide to do something, to act, and then apologize if things don't turn out as they should, if they fail and defeat comes, and the extreme and prolonged uncertainty of those who, on the other hand, before even thinking of moving an inch, must first ask permission and wait for approval from everyone. Doing is doing, and it moves things forward, and for better or worse, drives progress. Asking for permission is putting on the brakes, hiding behind an excuse (and we at Var Group are people with zero excuses, if you need to hear it again), it is staying sunk into your comfortable sofa waiting for perfection to rain down on you from above, as if by magic. Better to move forward than achieve perfection. Let's move forward in the meantime, we'll achieve perfection eventually. Let's do it, let's experiment, let's throw ourselves into it. With courage and audacity. *Progress over perfection.*

If we could find another way to balance autonomy and consistency, a way that does not necessarily involve a hierarchy based on positions of personal power, then we would hack the system. We would dismantle hierarchies and pyramid-shaped organization charts where conflict arises day in and day out because we continue to believe in false myths that have accompanied us since birth, according to which the more people report to you, the more power you have in the company. You hold an important position based on how many people you approve vacation time for. Or based on how high your box is. This is ephemeral power, which creates conflict instead of harmony, which pursues—at any cost—status, concepts, and the dictates of "those in charge."

Let's hack

Let's hack all this, and we'll be able to open the cage. Let's open the cage, and we'll have a completely different working environment. An environment where people listen to each other, listen to the context, and adapt continuously, both on a personal level and in relation to the organization. An environment where power goes where it's needed, but where it's really needed. In other words: where and when value can be generated or risk intercepted—things that often (if not always) happen on the periphery of the traditional system, i.e., precisely where the organization encounters the customer's needs. An environment where everyone can truly contribute. Where people feel good, where they feel better, and where they work better.

Var Group is a unique environment in which to do all this. Because it is growing, because it has grown so much over the years, and it has done so through acquisitions, welcoming into the Group companies that were already independent, thereby acquiring many different styles within itself.

Now a new era is dawning. It is time to find a way, a language, and processes to work better together. A new structure and new processes capable of balancing the coherence of the whole with the autonomy of each individual. Balancing everything, but always starting with people. In an open organization that can answer the question "Who is responsible for organizational change?" with "Literally everyone, all men and women," without any division between the company and the people who work there. Because those people *are* the company, and those people, that company, are us. It is therefore up to us to build the company we want to work in.

Var freestyle

Priel, as mentioned, is someone who connects things, and above all, people. His speech was also brief, and it couldn't have been otherwise in a Kick Off as different (or rather, as unique) as that of Maggio Fiorentino. It was short but got straight to the point, striking a chord with the audience because the story he told is our story. It was the daily bread for the entire population present, and for me, who for many years has had a dream: to structure and organize Var Group based on models of distributed leadership, where power is in the hands of all people. Priel's speech is the answer to a handful of questions that we had begun to ask ourselves more than a year ago, and which resonated in my head and in ours. Can it be done? Where to start? And how exactly to do it?

The goal is ambitious and far from guaranteed; it requires time, study, and experimentation. Especially in an organization as large as Var Group. The challenge defies all odds, because the chances of achieving such a goal, at this level and with this impact, are lower than the chances of failure. But we will do it, and we are already doing it. We are aware that "revolution is not a dinner party," to quote Mao, which opens Sergio Leone's epic film *Duck, You Sucker!*

We will do it, and we are already doing it in our own style, which is a free style in which every element is part of a larger message.

The result is not a simple sum. It cannot and must not be, especially in a company where power is in everyone's hands. In an addition, in fact, the result does not change if one of the numbers is zero. In Var, on the other hand, the result is a product, the result of a multiplication in which each individual is a factor and thus has the responsibility to contribute their own value, because even a single zero would cancel out the overall result.

At Var Group, we have a style that is all our own. It is not perfect, like everything else under the sun. But, if possible, it is something more, something better: it is human, and that makes all the difference in the world.

Vera

Then Vera arrives at Kick Off. Vera Gheno is a sociolinguist, as well as an essayist and activist. She talks to us about the meaning that words have in our lives. This is perhaps a difficult task in a context where the focus is mainly on technology. But perhaps the opposite is true, because language is also technology. In fact, it is one of the oldest forms of technology we have at our disposal and is still fundamental today, even though we live in an age universally considered to be the age of images. Because a picture is worth a thousand words. But which words?

An image, in fact, can be interpreted differently by each individual. Precision is therefore needed to share an accurate vision: words are needed, and words that are well chosen. To have well-chosen words, we must give the right importance to the technology of language. And, despite the results, we live in a world where we try to give importance to words. We study language extensively at school. Yet we never ask ourselves too many questions directly related to all this.

Why do we speak? Where does speech come from? How does language change? What do we do with words? Do we communicate? Certainly, but that is only part of the answer. The first thing we do is something private, personal. An individual act of identity. We are the words we choose to use. Or those we choose not to use. And we are also all the words that come out of our mouths at random, when life suggests that we are in a free port where we don't need to weigh every single word, with people who know us, whom we know, with whom we understand each other perfectly.

Future

At Var Group, we feel part of a large working family. That's why we have our own jargon to understand each other. We know how to "sniff each other out" a little within the organization, and this is very important, but we also define ourselves through our words. With our words, we try to understand who we are: we describe ourselves and can explain to others who we are and what we want. This is our individual identity. However, it does not fall into a cosmic void, because we always act among other people. With our words, we must therefore meet halfway to create a group, share the same linguistic code, and understand each other.

Every day, we use words to name reality. We are the only animals that know how to name things, and it is only after we have assigned a name to something that we can talk about it, and in doing so, make information "transportable." Other species only have the present, the here and now, and in order to communicate information, they must be together in the same place. We can talk to each other, send recordings, hear each other from a distance, write letters or books like the one you are holding in your hands right now, and we can read things written an infinite amount of time ago, such as the *Divine Comedy*. We can detach ourselves from the present and live in time. We can also detach ourselves from the place where we are and live in a diffuse manner. And we are the only living beings to have a dimension linked to the possession of speech. This dimension is the future. All other animals do not have, cannot have, the expectation of what will happen next.

When Covid hit us, the world, Italy, Tuscany, and Var Group, we tried to take remedial action to make up for everything that suddenly could no longer be done as before. We did so hastily, always keeping an eye on ensuring that no one felt isolated, alone, or helpless. We did so because we clearly felt that we were fighting against something that could take away our future.

Future perfect

With an uncertain future ahead of us, we began to thaw out a new dimension that went beyond a foggy, problematic, and infinitely distant tomorrow. With Covid, we dusted off the future perfect. Which is exactly what we got back once the storm had subsided. But a company that looks to the future must know how to narrate that future. And the technology of words, which paints today's challenges as those of tomorrow, serves precisely this purpose: to bring together people from different backgrounds, traditions, ages, prejudices, and judgments, for example.

As good human beings, we tend to love and stay with those who are like us. We don't really like having to relate to people who are very different from us. Every time we meet someone who is completely different from us, we automatically feel a little afraid, even anxious. But then we start to mediate and build a bridge. This mediation is possible thanks to words. Words can help us overcome the instinctive mistrust that every human being feels when faced with otherness. They can be a way of managing difference, of moving from an attitude of fear to one of curiosity.

To do this, we need to work on the technology of words. We need to be aware of how we use them, because everyone is an agent of change and, to quote the film director Nanni Moretti, "Words are important." We are responsible for the words we use and, to continue the round of quotes, bringing the cartoonist Zerocalcare into the mix, we must "shoulder" the consequences of our words, for better or for worse. And we must keep in mind that no two individuals in the world have the same linguistic baggage.

Pride and prejudice

Like DNA, our linguistic makeup is unique, apart from the fact that we have one thing in common, which is what allows us to be part of a whole. Our identity and our words are unique, but at the same time, they are part of the collective. Every word we choose to use is a drop falling into a pond: however small it may be, it generates a series of concentric circles. But the point is: we are always the architects of our linguistic stories.

Bringing people together from different backgrounds, traditions, and ages, as the history of our organization teaches us—including the many efforts we are making today to achieve a new model—is no joke, because it means finding the key to the puzzle when you discover that those people bring with them different prejudices and judgments. *Pride and prejudice* is not yet another bold reinterpretation of Jane Austen, but something much more practical, widespread, and everyday. Something we deal with more often than we would like, and more than we actually realize.

We live our lives keeping a series of biases and mental prejudices more or less at bay. My own story is one of open and relentless struggle against prejudice and stereotypes. A continuous struggle, I might add. Because those prejudices and stereotypical biases are everywhere, they are numerous and besiege us at all times, both personally and professionally. As a result, we always tend to listen not out of a desire to understand, but to limit ourselves to hearing, waiting (perhaps) for our turn, to then respond. This is as true for verbal language, for words, as it is for all other languages, primarily body language. That is why it is important to commit ourselves to understanding and explaining things correctly. Because in doing so, we build bridges that untangle the diversity of others and transform it into uniqueness.

Differences exist; the world is full of them. We believe that they work a bit like happiness in the words of Kurt Vonnegut: "I urge you to please notice when you are happy." Please notice when you are different. At Var Group, we embrace differences, because we need them to grow together.

It all started with a shoulder

Then the ball passes to Giovanni. That "Giovanni." Giovanni Moriani, who is here to create a synthesis, and to do so from a different point of view. Different because, year after year, he is less and less involved in operations. Different because he is increasingly able to look around him, to explore economic and technical issues in depth, and thus to make a real contribution to Var Group, which is now sailing towards a new frontier made up above all of new organizational models. But his point of view is also different for another reason. Because he begins by talking about his shoulder.

Giovanni fell and hurt himself on May 4, with the added complication that he was in Valencia, Spain. Six days later, on the 10th, he was home. He had undergone surgery, been discharged, and was able to do physical therapy. He had returned to Italy on Sunday evening and had asked for the names of a couple of reliable surgeons in Florence. Then he went on Google, logged onto a medical support management platform, and managed to get an appointment with his chosen surgeon for Tuesday morning. The surgeon saw him in a small public hospital and told him that he already had a list of operations for the following Thursday but that he could do it the next day, on Wednesday, although it would be a little complicated. At 7 a.m. on Wednesday morning, Giovanni received a WhatsApp message from the doctor, inviting him to go to the emergency room for a CT scan. While he was on his way to the hospital, he also received the estimate for the private practice fee, which he confirmed by email and paid online. He arrived at the hospital, where the surgeon, seeing that the paperwork was complete, told him that in addition to the CT scan, he would also be admitted to the hospital, without even sending him home and making him come back. At 1 p.m., Giovanni was sent to the ward, with the operation scheduled for 6 a.m. the following morning. The next day, he wrote to the surgeon, again on WhatsApp, to confirm that he was feeling well and already in a condition to return home.

The surgeon had come to see him at the end of the operation, examined him, and suggested that he request the diskette from the regional platform to present to the physical therapist. The moral of the story: 48 hours later, Giovanni left with the diskette under his arm (the healthy one!) to go to the physical therapist and arrange the necessary rehabilitation. All through the public health system. And all thanks to digital technology.

This is a small experience recounted by Giovanni at the Kick Off, but small experiences teach us a lot. And this one teaches us that digital technology can make a difference, both in organization and in everyday life.

Work, share, grow

Small experiences teach big lessons, but many people are still completely unaware of this. They are amazed that platforms exist, that they can be used in this way, that things and flows can be managed digitally, and that all this can really be a great advantage, not in itself and for most systems, but in concrete terms and for everyone. Digital technology, innovation, models: all this is just waste paper if there is nothing behind it. If there are no people. Because people are the foundation of a company and its organizational models, and even more so with their culture, insofar as the organizational models we are talking about must become self-determining.

Everyone must work on their own culture and according to their previous experiences in order to share it and help it grow. However, looking around, we realize that it is still very difficult to grow culturally in the direction of embracing a digital life, which for us at Var Group is both a mission and a job. Culture is a fundamental element, because without a shared culture it is difficult to cultivate creativity, and in a new organization that wants to be self-determined, we have an imperative to be creative. But without a shared culture behind it, all creativity becomes distorted and ends up being an end in itself, nothing more than a sterile intuition.

The Times They Are A-Changin'

The Times They Are A-Changin'. Times have changed, to quote Bob Dylan. Times are different. Compared to the past, what has changed is that before there was time to adapt, and in such a context, even if you had to deal with undisciplined people, it wasn't really a big deal in the end. In fact, their way of doing things could give you new ideas to take on, and in any case, it was a way, albeit an unconventional one, of "making change."

Now there is no time left for any of that. Because if before there was a whole season to play, between obtaining players, preparing, planning and executing, today the rules are made overnight. And they keep changing. Therefore, if you focus on a self-generated model, there must be discipline in that model, otherwise you risk losing efficiency. It's true, mistakes happen anyway – and when they do, they must be corrected as soon as possible – but that doesn't mean you don't need immediate discipline, because time is the scarcest resource in our world. A world that is awash with organizations that have spent time, effort and resources planning major organizational changes for their people, their workspaces, their workflow, only to find themselves halfway through and witness the shipwreck of all the change simply because the rules of the game have changed in the meantime.

That is why we must protect a shared culture, bold creativity, and why not, rigorous discipline: to allow people themselves, and the new organizational models that Giovanni defines as "self-generated," to constantly adapt to a market that is just as constantly changing its skin and rules.

Today, tomorrow morning, and beyond

When Giovanni takes the stage, one thing always happens: the entire audience looks at him, seeking his gaze. To remind him of the same recommendation one always gives to a visionary: strive to be concise! In that glance, in seeking a reassuring look that tells us that yes, he will do his best to stay on schedule, lies one of the most deeply rooted traditions of our Kick Off. It happens at the Maggio Fiorentino as well. It happens, and it continues while he speaks, thinks, and speaks again. It happens, and in the end it is he himself who decides to reassure us, sprinkling information throughout his speech that answers our doubts.

In the end, it all comes back to people. Because to rethink paradigms, I need them: people. People who share a culture that, despite generations, despite backgrounds, despite everything, grows, moves forward, and takes shape day after day. And then creativity, boldness, and discipline. But also something else.

The last note with which Giovanni closes his speech is the ability to dream. Because we must keep one eye fixed on the present, on the immediate future, but we must also be able to give ourselves a purpose, to go beyond. It is by dreaming that people give themselves that goal. Something to achieve. Something they believe is worth striving for, worth doing. And dreams are important because they give satisfaction. They give satisfaction when you find them. They give satisfaction when you work on them. And they give the most satisfaction when they are achieved. Dreaming is the only way to actually change things to our full satisfaction. The world needs people who are capable of dreaming. We need people who are capable of dreaming. Because people dream at all ages. And we must never stop.

One fine day, in the best economics textbooks

Before the party-party-party begins, when we throw ourselves headlong into an ocean of collective intelligence in our usual crazy and daring way, there is the official closing of the Kick Off. At the Maggio Fiorentino, once his speech is over, Giovanni starts to leave the stage, but he is stopped and brought back to the center, together with the crowd of colleagues who co-hosted the event (Victoria Cabello, an "adopted Var-groupie," was the host) or by speakers who took the stage during the two hours to illustrate the projects they are working on.

I go up last, partly because everything I have experienced in those 120-plus minutes, added to the pre- and post-excitement, is something that makes me feel unsteady. I go up, thank everyone, and announce the last three things, promising to be quick so as not to delay the celebrations any further. "Stop, and celebrate," says the wise man who has become a voice in my head. And so I go with my three things, which are actually Var Group's 2025 goals, and above all three things that belong to the entire audience.

I'll start with the most obvious one. 900 million in revenue. People's eyes widen. I can read their lips: "Obvious???" And I add: "Obvious, in the sense that revenue is a consequence of everything we do on a daily basis." I don't think I need to say anything else.

The second objective, which by now will be well known since we have gone over it countless times and from many different angles: investing, believing, and dreaming in a change of organizational model. This is extremely important to me and to everyone. So much so that we are working together, not only to create it, but also to make it work. In other words, to ensure that one day it ends up in economics textbooks.

Have fun, in 2024

Then the peak comes. There was a time when Var Group's first, only, and most important goal was something I had to shout out loud... It wasn't that long ago, but it feels like a lifetime. It was a time of change, maybe, when there was still a long way to go, obstacles to overcome, lessons to learn, and things to figure out.

Today, many things have changed, perhaps, here as well. Or perhaps they have only changed in form, because the concept has remained the same, identical, and unchanging: the number one goal is still "HAVE FUN!" It has become a leitmotif for everyone at Var, in every language, since I have personally worked hard to spread it in Germany, Spain, and Romania. I have said it so many times, and in so many different languages, that this initial goal is now firmly rooted in everyone's mind. It is one of those things that is said first after being hired.

That's the official "fun." Because after Var Group's Kick Off, there are many other Kick Offs, each related to a business unit or a specific team. I participate in all of them, one by one. Because that imperative deserves an adequate explanation. Because having fun is not just "let's go out for a drink and celebrate *afterwards*." I am eager to convey the notion that having fun is "having fun while you work." It's getting out of bed in the morning knowing that you have to go to work, but that you'll also have fun doing it. Going through the various vertical Kick Offs, the "children" of the Group Kick Off, means explaining what needs to be done, applying the concept of fun to the specific work of individual companies, BUs, and teams.

It's true, having fun also means organizing lots of parties, with good food and an open bar. It means listening to music and dancing until late. And we do all of this. With satisfaction, too, given that, as I was saying, what are perhaps our best ideas have come from the collective intelligence unleashed during evenings of "free time." This is also part of having fun. But it can't be just this. It has to be something that enters the office.

So my ambition is to create environments and an organizational context where there is also fun, but together with elements such as discipline and motivation. Environments and contexts where people feel good and work with peace of mind.

Curtains

That said, after that "Have fun!" I always start to feel like when the bell rings on the last day of school. Only a little more excited, if possible. At that moment, as we start hugging each other on stage and rallying the audience to their feet because the final moment of the event is about to begin, time slows down for me, but only for a moment. Because there is still so much to do, starting tomorrow. But for today, for now, and for tonight, there's still fuel to burn. We step aside, get off the stage, and it no longer feels like a corporate event. Because, in fact, it was never "just" a corporate event.

It seems like something else. A concert. The stage vibrates, the lights vibrate, the Maggio Fiorentino vibrates, and we vibrate too. At the beginning, Mario Winans' *I Don't Wanna Know* resounds (which recalls and samples the hook from the Fugees' *Ready or Not*). But we're just warming up. Then *Empire State of Mind*, *Halo* by Beyoncé and even *New York, New York* complete with soprano. And when everything goes dark again, that's exactly when the guitars start rumbling. I sway to *Are You Gonna Go My Way?* by the immortal Lenny Kravitz. I dance to *I Can't Get No (Satisfaction)* by the Stones. And then, then I go wild when the Stones fade away and we find ourselves dealing with *Highway to Hell* by AC/DC. And we continue, together, until the grand finale. And then, then there's just the curtain.

The birth of the heavy cloud

When I decided to write this chapter, having started the story with a Preface, I thought I would stick faithfully to the plot line and end with an Epilogue. But it didn't work. Because an epilogue, since the beginning of time, is meant to represent the conclusion of a story. If I had kept this title, I would not have done justice to my story, nor to that of Var Group, which is the story of many people who, together with me, take it a few inches further every day.

That's why I put quotation marks around it. Because this is a clear and vibrant snapshot of a story that intertwines us, and that not only does not end here but also has plenty of fuel left to burn. Everything you find in these pages is already happening and will continue to happen, because if we want to get straight to the heart of innovation, we have to think "like innovation," behave like it behaves, be like it. And innovation, by definition, knows no epilogues.

I told you; I even wrote it down. To recount in detail everything that went on inside, behind, and around the Maggio Fiorentino Kick Off, an entire book would be needed, and a thick one at that. In these pages, I have stuck to the big picture and what most catches the eye, trying to convey to you, the readers, as much as possible, what I felt. I have cut and deleted a lot. But what remains, in line with the aims that inspired the book you hold in your hands, is a huge cloud. Full of ideas, projects, construction sites, and commitments that I and the whole Var Group have conceived, planned, launched, and developed, with the sole aim of making the Var Group of the future worthy of the dream that is ours.

That cloud will soon give birth, and in fact it is already doing so. The birth of such a heavy cloud is a heavy rain, which falls and will fall on our heads, making this ecosystem look like a company, a group, an organization to many; but for us, myself first of all, it is infinitely more, infinitely different. Because it represents the intersection between life and work. And if everyone can aspire to a better life, because that is the right of every individual, with the courage, daring, discipline, and motivation that they can muster, using the exact same ingredients, we are aiming for a new Var Group, even more capable of moving straight toward a direction that is obviously at the heart of innovation.

"The" Challenge

I want to break free

1984 was a turbulent year. Apple launched the first Macintosh, the police caught the Ludwig gang of serial killers, and earthquakes shook the Italian regions of Umbria, Abruzzi, Latium, and Molise. A parliamentary commission began to officially lift the veil on the secret P2 Masonic lodge, Italian Communist Party leader Enrico Berlinguer suffered a serious illness from which he would not recover, and mafia informant Tommaso Buscetta's statements nailed an octopus with 366 arrest warrants. The IRA planted a bomb in what would become "my" Brighton, the Soviets launched Vega 2 to take a look at Venus and Halley's Comet, and Japan launched *Dragon Ball*. Ups and downs. Then there was the music. Pupo and Matia Bazar, *Axel F* providing the soundtrack to *Beverly Hills Cop*. David Bowie with *Blue Jean*, and *Dancing in the Dark* by the "Boss" Bruce Springsteen.

And, once again, *I want to break free*. Queen was lost, navigating one of the toughest moments of their artistic life: behind them, the semi-failure of their previous album, which included *Under Pressure* but also too much dance music; ahead of them, a tour in South Africa that would prove to be another gauntlet. Queen in 1984 was a band at a crossroads, no ifs, no buts about it. Either they would choose to throw it all away, since they literally couldn't stand each other anymore, or they would grit their teeth, rack their brains to find a balance between 1980s dance music and their rock pedigree, and carry on. They chose option two—or the second door, if we want to stay true to the lyrics of that song—and the result was phenomenal. One of the best fruits of this decision was that very song, with its yearning, repeated until the very last verse, to free themselves from lies and constraints, get back on their feet, walk through the door, and away. *I Want to Break Free* is a song for all seasons, in the sense that it plays on a need, that of returning to savor freedom, which is so familiar that it can become a tribute to anyone. Perhaps this is why it is one of the most misunderstood songs ever. In any case, in the chaos with which we closed the previous chapter, which literally transformed a "corporate event" into a big concert, I think it would have been perfect!

A table too short

Above all because it fully embodies, in its extreme simplicity, a desire I have always had and always tried to fulfill: to have an organization where people feel truly and fully free. Free to express themselves transparently. It was a big gamble to take. You can only accept a gamble like that if there are many hands involved in managing it.

It was a long time ago, practically a Var Group ago. At the time, I had people close to me, Var Group front-liners and leaders, if we had to classify them in some way. I felt that drive, and I really wanted to convey those concepts. So, I started a series of meetings.

Those leadership meetings were specifically designed to give us the opportunity and time to discuss things. To look each other in the face and open the way for thoughts and proposals. However, the table was always, invariably, short because there were only a few of us. Four or five, and no more. Then we always ended up somehow off track, because the perspective we could apply, which came almost automatically, was that of four or five figures from top management; as such, it worked well as a perspective, from above and in a certain sense from a bird's eye view, but it was extremely difficult to glide and land. In other words, it was difficult to develop something that went beyond the vision itself and became a concrete reality that could be put into practice. Things were reaching a breaking point. And it was taking us back to the years before Covid in a long trail that went back to the earlier years. Before 2020, there were other tables at Var Group, managed by Giovanni, where the dynamic was always the same: he spoke and the others listened.

Chinese whispers

In 2020, that already overly classic structure had inevitably collapsed onto itself. And, once safe conditions for people and the greatest possible continuity of operations had been hastily ensured, other tables had somehow reappeared on their own, different from before and reflecting a broader need: to maintain, even if only virtually, a thread of hope and sharing with all the people who were used to considering the office an important part of their days, not only in terms of work, but also in terms of their very identity.

Small work tables where, however, there was always the same glue: yours truly. First I would talk to one person, then another, and then I would connect the dots. It was tiring, personally speaking, and required an unusual amount of energy and attention to detail, memory, and diplomacy. Above all, this tendency presented a "mechanical" problem that could not be ignored: it was a stop-start process which, like the classic Chinese whispers game, slowed down the discussion as it had to pass through a series of important and complex steps.

So, with Covid somehow behind us and 2021 once again demanding a response to that desire for freedom, I decided that enough was enough. That the "short table" had to remain a thing of the past. Just like the "emergency micro-tables" which, having been created during the pandemic, had the added limitation of having been tested in the only way possible at the time: online and without any physical presence. Both had had their day. If we really wanted change and innovation, if I wanted and we wanted to have any real chance of succeeding in making a real impact, the table had to be expanded, both physically and conceptually.

Var Talks

Meanwhile, time continued to pass inexorably. The gradual return to a kind of "normality" in 2021 was followed by 2022. And I continued to feel the cracks in this method. This was also because, in the meantime, Var Group had grown, and grown a lot. We had bet everything on one card. And in the end, we had to deal with Babylon. A place where the only rule was that there were no rules, and which at a certain point had plunged us into organizational chaos.

In October 2022, something happened. Not in the world, but in my head. I realized that I was spending too much time thinking about the "table" itself, as a format. By doing so, I was limiting my intuition. And I was literally missing out on a whole series of stimuli that had the "limitation" of coming from totally different contexts and which, as such, I discarded simply because they were not directly related to what I was looking for. The biggest of these stimuli came from TED talks. Which—look how small the world is—were born in the same year as *I Want to Break Free,* 1984.

TED stands for Technology Entertainment Design, and the first TED talks were nothing more than single events, later becoming annual conferences dedicated to technology and design. TED caused quite a stir, starting in Silicon Valley and quickly spreading like wildfire, both geographically and thematically, becoming practically a cult phenomenon. The idea behind TED was brilliant: to be a place where ideas "absolutely worth spreading" could come to life. The same intuition was behind the new "table" format that I wanted to develop for Var Group. That's how I came up with the name Var Talks: meetings of our leadership team, but designed and structured to become real working groups.

Freedom, too much freedom?

These were moments when we would get together to come up with things to do. In the early days, like all totally experimental projects, Var Talks were very much a work in progress. This was mainly because they were approached—more or less unconsciously—in the same way as previous discussions, where one person spoke and the rest of the group listened and, at most, took notes.

That was the first hurdle to overcome. And I had decided to tackle it head-on. Of course, I had decided who should be at the table and prepared the agenda, but when it came down to it, I limited myself to facilitating the meeting, listening while the rest of the group was free to speak.

And here another issue emerged. After seasons of unidirectionality that had culturally convinced everyone that they should only listen, that part of the table, once invested with the autonomy to speak, seemed a little uncomfortable with all that freedom in their hands. This meant that they spoke, of course, but also that the dynamic was often limited to a rigid and orderly presentation, one of those where you first make your introduction, then the institutional moment of discussion begins, and so on. We held the first Var Talk strictly in-house, in Empoli. I will always remember it, not only because it was the first, but also and above all because it was an opportunity to introduce ourselves.

"Hi, I'm X and I do Y." Introducing yourself in the most literal sense of the word. Because all those outdated, partial, and emergency attempts that had been tried in previous years had always relied on an extremely limited number of participants. So now there was a real need to start from scratch. Introducing yourself, because the people, except for me, didn't know each other at all. It must be said, for the record, that projects were born and ideas were flowing. Carefully, we identified each one, assigned ownership to each idea, and started working on them.

This modus operandi, which was certainly not perfect, was definitely the best we could achieve at the time. As such, it had been through its baptism of fire and had also had a few good months to be broken in. Months in which, with our diaries in hand, we would find a couple of days to meet up and start working thanks to common sense, without any precise ritual to organize everything.

Mayday

It held up, it worked. The problem was "how." Because, at a certain point, we were plagued by a series of Hamlet-like doubts. Were we really working? And was our organization working too? Those questions, those doubts did not arise randomly or suddenly. Behind them lay a sense of fatigue that we were beginning to feel and understand was directly related to our approach to innovation, which was certainly generous but also totally disorganized and, for this very reason, exhausting in the long run.

It was at that point that Mirko began to point out that perhaps, given that even the solution we had tried to implement was reaching a dead end, we needed to put other minds to it. This was especially necessary because the projects that came out of Var Talks were created by those who had ownership and developed proposals, and they all had what it took to achieve the goal, which was to build the future of the organization piece by piece. The result was by no means to be discarded, but we urgently needed to find someone to help us bring order to the method, get it up and running, and in this way spread leadership beyond Var Talks and throughout the entire company: this was the clear dream in our minds, the spearhead of tomorrow's Var Group.

If power belongs to everyone at Var Group, then everyone has the opportunity to find a solution. But throwing ourselves wholeheartedly into this new quest would have been carnage, especially at a time when things were exploding around us. We had decided to start two channels of research; different, and if possible opposite, so as to obtain a wide variety of options from which to choose. On one side was Mirko, on the other Maurizio. Mirko started from the theme of power in the hands of all people. He studied and studied, and came up with a model, a "social technology" as its founder Brian Robertson calls it, which expressed precisely that concept, *holacracy*, which emanated from a strong principle of self-organization. And he tracked down Kopernicana, one of the few organizations in Italy that was working concretely in that direction.

Maurizio, on the other hand, starting from more "lofty" and superstructural assumptions, and at the end of his personal (and different) research opted to recommend a large consulting firm, well-structured and therefore more experienced in offering support to Var Group to make its "dreams of glory" come true. On one side, the established player; on the other, the underdog. We called them both in at different times but on the same fateful date: February 14, 2023. For the rest of the world, it was probably just another Valentine's Day. For us, it was the moment of truth.

The Valentine's Day of truth

The big day had arrived, and the established player was the first to present their case. They brought us a well-established, clear-cut model in which, in exchange for an offer that cost a fortune, they claimed that within a year they would put us in a position to ride the tiger. The underdog arrived more quietly, with a totally different approach. First of all, they presented themselves in tandem with a partner with a proven track record in creating innovative places to support talent in digital and technology, and who, at that very moment, was extensively involved in their operations. Then they started explaining things, and things, and things. All of which were correct, agreeable, and sacrosanct. But they didn't seem to go into any depth as to "how" all those principles would then be translated into reality in our daily lives.

We listened, took note of everything, thanked them, and said good-bye. Immediately afterwards, Var Talk met to analyze everything, give shape and breadth to our impressions, and agree on a line of action and a choice. Needless to say, most of us were inclined to accept the proposal of the "big" player. It was a good proposal, no doubt about it. Or at least, it was on paper. There were questions, there were answers, there were dynamics, there was everything. A scale model of the future. It was a good system. Perhaps too good. Too good to be applied to the letter. Too good because, as I had learned, life is never linear. And so, wherever some form of perfect accuracy is peddled, I automatically have serious doubts.

The big player's proposal was "perfect" on that exact scale. As such, I struggled to see it implemented as it was, *tout court*, by us. To tell the truth, I struggled to see it implemented in any specific case. But it certainly didn't convince me in ours, which was the case of a company that was anything but perfect. And yet it wanted to become, and still wants to become, completely human. Add to that the fact that I had also taken the time, together with Mirko, to have a face-to-face chat with Kopernicana, the underdog, and in doing so we had also gained several additional insights, which we now had to weigh up.

Enormous value, enormously different

In the end, the underdog prevailed. With a bit of banging fists on the table, for the record. Perfecting a choice that is still paying off today. In the meantime, to address the need for support in facilitation, which we believed to be the Achilles' heel of the Var Talks at the time, we brought in Talent Ward, the corporate university that provides training for people at Var Group and which actively facilitated three editions of Var Talks, allowing us to make progress in our mutual understanding and to agree on activities to be developed rigorously together.

Then the baton of facilitation was officially passed to Kopernicana, and many things took shape with them. We began to define rituals, to use tensions as opportunities for improvement for the leadership team, to actively pursue projects and initiatives that, since then, have remained a common heritage on which we continue to work, together and in a way that multiplies the results of our "simple" efforts. Var Talk has thus found its way, an evolutionary path, growing in diversity and numbers: today, it involves the participation of nineteen leaders representing business units or shared service platforms, i.e., organizations within the Var Group system that provide enabling services to other units. What's more, the entrepreneurs, who are always men, have joined the Group following acquisitions and are an excellent counterbalance to the managerial "front." It is precisely from the active coexistence of these two points of view—different in themselves, but also and above all in their approach to the world of business—that we are able to generate enormous value, which is vastly different from what any competitor "traditionally" can or knows how to do.

Now, by defining entrepreneurs on one side and managers on the other, I am actually exaggerating the concept. I am doing so, contrary to my strictly anti-stereotypical nature, both in fact and in position, with the sole aim of simplifying the explanation, in the face of a real world in which there are infinite different and nuanced gradations between the two "pure categories."

"The problem of the company"

Take the world of management, for example. For years, I heard senior managers repeat ad nauseam that managers were "the problem of the company." In truth, as I saw it and experienced it, what I can say about this is that, perhaps, there are two macrocosms when it comes to managers: managers who are born to execute, on the one hand, and managers who have the vision necessary to design strategies, on the other. Neither is "the problem," I want to make that clear right away.

The "problem," if we really want to call it that, lies elsewhere, further upstream. The problem of a company is when we are unable to understand exactly how much of each approach is necessary within the organization. A manager in and of themselves is not problematic. On the contrary, they are essential because, if they are a true manager, they have an entrepreneurial mindset, not just gut instinct, which allows them to see the strategy on the one hand, but also to understand how to execute it on the other.

Then, to state the harsh reality, it is equally true that there are managers who have a deep entrepreneurial spirit, as well as those who do business with a managerial mindset. If I had to define myself, I would not be able to give you a complete answer, but only an impression, plus another corollary. In fact, I have the entirely personal impression that I feel more like a manager, but very often I am described—this is the "social" impression—as an entrepreneur.

With all the nuances that life can bring, as mentioned, experiences channel you in the direction of one universe or the other. Similarly, with all the nuances of life and previous experiences, today's Var Talk features people who have dedicated their entire lives to entrepreneurship, as well as people who have followed a managerial logic throughout their lives in other companies. But the real point is and remains that, beyond the great distinction between them—and perhaps precisely because of their coexistence, which triggers an exceptional contrast that is at the basis of every artistic concept—beyond this and thanks to this, the union of the two different points of view is fundamental for Var Group. It works wonderfully. And it's worth the price of admission, which is exactly the measure of the patience to ensure that these two identities, so different yet so strategic in a chessboard like ours, understand each other.

Beyond Taylor, beyond Ford

We went through a terrible period. As I have already told you, the desire for "total" freedom and to follow the one rule of doing away with rules altogether had unleashed anarchy, which was devouring the company. The paradox was that, in the meantime, turnover and EBITDA were growing. But also, and above all, that internally, people were starting to feel uncomfortable, and externally, our reference market was beginning to show signs of dissatisfaction. In search of a solution, we began looking for an alliance with someone who had the ability to do what we couldn't or didn't yet know how to do.

In Kopernicana, we found the right partner to help us unravel the mystery, understand the situation, and offer us the tools to take action and put things into practice. At the same time, our internal academy began working closely with our ally, Talent Ward and Kopernicana together, establishing a sort of supply chain in which the practices of the second player became the training provided by the first. In this supply chain, the second player shaped the tools for designing a new organizational model, and the first built targeted paths on top of it so that people could ride the wave of change without being overwhelmed.

When I write "new organizational model," when I say it and repeat it in my speeches, including the one at the Kick Off at Maggio Fiorentino, I don't do it by chance. I do so because I have long recognized that the world has changed in every way: socially, economically, industrially, and technologically. The world has changed, driven by a crazy evolution. And that same evolution has shattered every previous paradigm. I ask myself: if this is true, how can we hope to figure it out when in some areas we continue to judge the world and things through outdated lenses, sometimes even dusting off Taylorism or Fordism?

In the hope of being contradicted

I ask this question both to myself and to other people wherever possible. I do so in the hope of being contradicted. But every time, the result is the same. Old models are still being studied, even though everyone knows in their heart of hearts that their day has passed. The challenge, then, is to ensure that universities can begin to study something different, a new organizational model that I would very much like to see born, grow, and be tested at Var Group.

I am referring to a model that finally kicks out everything that is outdated but still followed and insisted upon today: antediluvian divisions of labor, invented in an industrial or even proto-industrial world, which had built its path to efficiency and productivity through command and control, inevitably sacrificing the ability of workers to see value, and with it, the very possibility for each individual to contribute with initiative, intelligence, and responsibility. Or, taking it one step further, creating new professional figures who, from a certain point in history onwards, manage, plan, and control work with the mission of finding, on a scientific basis, the "one best way"—as Taylor put it—the only way to do that exact piece of work and define the corresponding task to be assigned to those working at that moment.

I can't stand that companies are still shaped by a model, cobwebs included, originally conceived in an era when, in what would today be a slap in the face to the concept of customer focus, it was possible to say that a Model T could come in "Any color the customer wants, as long as it's black." That's history, or at least it should be. It should be because, in reality, on many, too many points, nothing has changed.

In the vast majority of cases, it is probably only the way we represent the company graphically that has changed. But the underlying concept remains the same: make a profit and hold on to it. Others would say: *exploit*, rather than *explore*. Against all this, and against much else besides, beyond this outdated model that is unsuited to our times, we need a new model.

Oxymorons

A new model cannot be created overnight. Behind it, as Giovanni said at the Maggio Fiorentino, there needs to be a culture. The culture of people: of all people, both those in charge and those who must obey (forgive the categorical simplifications). To work on the culture of all people, training is needed, a lot of it, and a lot of practice. Because we have become very accustomed to certain organizational models. And, more or less consciously, we end up expecting things like hierarchy, command and control, the handing out of tasks (which we mistakenly call responsibility) that, once received, we don't know where to start managing and exercising.

My primordial desire to arrive at a situation where the only rule was the absolute absence of rules was completely wrong. I experienced it firsthand, through sweat and wounds that I still bear on my back, and we experienced it throughout the entire company. I was wrong in good faith, because what I was aiming for was a sudden reversal that would establish an open organization. The intention was good, but unfortunately the execution was not. Above all, because it ignored one of those elements that fully belong to the category of "things I realized too late": a truly open organization works under one condition: if there are clear and shared rules behind it. Rules that are concrete and at the same time modifiable, but clear to everyone.

Put in these terms, it is a beautiful oxymoron. How can an organization function in an open mode if there are rules that, by definition, should limit openness itself? In reality, the reason is quite simple and has a lot to do with the culture of permission that we mentioned earlier.

If you can clearly explain what can and cannot be done, you are actually doing at least two other things. The first and most obvious is that you are creating a barrier to total anarchy. The second, that you are creating a safe perimeter within which people are finally and truly free to act. I have said it before and I will say it again: freedom thrives on boundaries, enabling limits that literally empower people to act.

In any case, it all depends on how the rules are written. And this is precisely one of the most important areas we are working on today. Because those rules must have a specific set of characteristics; it is not enough to take a handful at random and make them enforceable. First of all, they must not be written by Francesca Moriani, who decides that these are the rules for everyone at Var Group, period. Rather, there must be people behind them who have to act on those rules on a daily basis, because only in this way will they make sense beyond any specific case or more or less unambiguous point of view. And then, they must be balanced with all the necessary attention. This means: not too many, otherwise we will be back to not being able to do anything. They must be clear and understandable. They must be written down and accessible to every single individual, because everyone must be able to observe them with complete transparency. They must include meta-rules for modifying them, where necessary, inspired by a simple principle that we have learned from a management system known as Sociocracy: "good enough for now, safe enough to try." Open organization stems from this type of rules, which are progressive and imperfect by design.

Then there is at least one other potential oxymoron to bear in mind when trying to grow an open organization. For such a model to become an objective reality, it requires leaders who inspire with great force—contrary to mere common sense, according to which open organizations should have people in charge who are equally open-minded and unconventional, even to the point of laxity. But leaders with great strength here do not mean that they have to rule in a despotic and authoritarian manner. It means something we have already encountered in the previous pages: figures who know how to facilitate. Personally, I sometimes see myself a bit like *Nanny 911*. In the best (and least offensive) sense of the term: a support figure who, rather than just feeding the child, teaches them how to use a fork. My goal, my obsession, my daily hope is to create the conditions for people to learn to move, to learn to act, to learn. That's why I insist on training. That's why we invest so much in this area. Training, training, training. Which becomes practice, practice, practice.

Speaking of roles...

Furthermore, there is a whole lot of hard work involved, which does not concern the people themselves, but rather the definition of roles. A person is not a role; it does not work like in elections, where one head equals one vote. In life, as in work, we play and can play multiple roles at the same time. A woman can easily be both a mother and a partner. Or, a single role can be played by several different people. Every game has a referee, and in every game the referee is a different person.

In hierarchical organizations, there is always a great deal of confusion that associates the power of the role with the person, so to speak, crushing them into that role and relegating everything that person is to the narrow space of an organization chart box. This is not only reductive, but also unrealistic, if we just think about the fact that a person working in a company, even the most mediocre one, actually does many different things at the same time, very few of which actually fit into a "box."

We aim to unlock the power of the role and give it breathing room. Because, as we see it (and as we teach the practices of open organizations, such as the aforementioned holacracy) a role is a mix of three components. One is *purpose*. One of our fundamental principles is that every role must have its own purpose. If you think about it, this is a radical departure from the norm. In every self-respecting company, since the dawn of time, a great deal of work has been done to define the purpose, but that same tireless work, at best, stops at the purpose of the company as a whole. Stop. No purpose for the BUs, no purpose for the teams, no purpose for those within the company, within a BU, and within a team. Var Group cannot afford such naivety. Especially since it has chosen, since we have chosen, to tackle such a big issue as open organization head-on.

With a truly clear and heartfelt purpose, a couple of things happen. One is automatic: many rules disappear on their own because they prove less necessary when the purpose finally becomes explicit. The other is that you can move on to the second constituent element of the role itself: the expectations to which you respond, the "accountabilities." These are varied and represent things that the system expects from that role on a regular basis.

And then, to complete the triad, there is the domain. This represents an area of exclusive ownership that cannot be touched by other roles: if the role is, for example, that of social media manager, a domain could be access to social channels and the publication of content.

HR construction site

A purpose for every role – and nothing less. With a set of associated expectations that clearly define what the company expects that role to do, and a domain of ownership: what the role is solely responsible for and empowered to carry out independently. This is one of the fundamental issues we are pursuing today, the exercise we are undertaking, one of the construction sites underway, in an way that absolutely cuts across different sectors; one of many, incidentally. By "construction site," I mean literally: a place where the organization is working on itself, improving itself, with the same progressive and localized logic that we see in the construction sites scattered throughout our cities. We have vertical construction sites, on every BU, and horizontal construction sites, such as those involving the entire world of HR.

With a fundamental effort to make amends, on a personal level. For years, I considered Human Resources to be a function straddling the line between bureaucracy and administration. An evolved version, but not too much, of the classic "payroll and social contributions." I was convinced of this because, for me, it was totally wrong that HR, which I saw as far removed from the actual business, could interact and talk to people. Instead, I believed that people should talk to their "leaders." It was an incomplete and totally naive point of view. Naive because I only later began to understand that, in reality, people are sometimes not entirely comfortable talking to their "boss." Especially if they have to deal with something that concerns that person specifically. There is always an underlying double fear: that speaking up will lead to retaliation, in a specific sense; and that creating mechanisms for dialogue of this kind is nothing more than a trap to expose "dissidents" and ensure that they are "purged" in some way. This double fear is the result of a specific, erroneous, and deeply rooted cultural legacy. Instead, a respectable organization should cultivate (and lead to) a culture of feedback, in which judgment is eliminated in favor of transparency and in which, if there is something I don't like about you, I am free to come and tell you as it is, because you will not be offended but, on the contrary, you will listen to me, you will understand me, and together, or with the mediation of a colleague, we will manage any conflict (because, in fact, life between people is also, and very much so, made up of conflicts).

The "limited" HR that was in my head has been revised, even drastically. Today, there is not just a team, but a real HR community. A community in which, given that HR lives close to the business, there are a series of HR business partners dedicated to each BU. With such a community, the HR team can share practices and avoid ending up working just on their own, which would ultimately result in a cloud of totally different and unrelated initiatives. The community harmonizes everything HR does because it does not operate in silos, but as a horizontal, broad platform; and because it works "on site," facilitated by Kopernicana, with the aim of setting its own rules and becoming the architect of its own direct functioning.

DEI construction site

Another working group is dedicated to Diversity, Equity, and Inclusion. It was 2023, Kick Off again, when I launched an appeal from the stage to establish a team of Var Group ambassadors on issues related to diversity. To our surprise, and far exceeding our already optimistic expectations, within a short time eighty people volunteered and spontaneously applied to take up this challenge. The journey began, the first phase has been completed, and we have also found a way to develop it further. We will continue to develop and replicate it, because DEI presents a challenge that we cannot afford to ignore or lose.

Diversity is not just an issue that concerns women and men. It is not just about religion. It is not just about skin color. Above all, it aims to value uniqueness. Because we, as people, are all different from one another due to the conditioning we have experienced in our personal lives, in our families, the opportunities that life has given us, and as a consequence, the skills we have developed from these experiences. We differ in everything, and everything is diversity.

This journey, for its part, seeks to highlight how important it is to devote time and effort to valuing uniqueness, while also trying to manage any biases we may have naturally have, and to which we are naturally exposed and subject.

"Ambassadors" and "allies" are not just symbolic figures. For us, they are also a means to an end. A means to reach even the most difficult places, sending messages to areas of the company that are traditionally less exposed and, as such, more difficult to access. These are "peripheral" jobs—but it is often in the periphery that new things happen—which perhaps operate more quietly and are less widely known. We must find a way to get these messages across there as well. That is why ambassadors and allies are present in different territories and in the various BUs, as well as in all the companies of the Group. Needless to say, the entire HR team is also involved.

OKRs

Var Talk itself is a work in progress, constantly evolving. We have established and consolidated regular rituals that punctuate our agenda: weekly Friday morning video calls, with an hour set aside to decide what to talk about, tools in hand: the presentation of a project or a tension (where "tension" is a technical term used in holacracy to indicate a mismatch, a discrepancy between the current state of a role and what it tends towards, its purpose or accountability. Tension, in essence, is anything that prevents me from fully energizing my role and that generates a need. In fact, "What do you need?" is the question that the facilitator ritually asks those present at the meetings): the two-hour monthly meeting, always on video, which hosts more substantive retrospectives; and then, last but not least, the two-day in-person meeting held every two months, where the real magic takes place. And so, often and willingly, big things happen.

One example is useful above all others: the first draft of our OKRs (Objectives and Key Results), which are an extremely important framework for guiding strategy throughout the entire organization. We put the OKRs down on paper in a Var Talk and from there decided to start a process of "cascading," i.e., the dissemination of strategic writing, throughout the Var Group during the next Var Talk, with a parallel, connected, and synergistic project, according to which, precisely in view of the cascading, 168 people from various leadership teams have completed OKR training, preparing the ground for further cascading. It's crazy, perhaps; certainly courageous. And being bold and boldly creative, with the discipline we have guaranteed ourselves, it is just as certainly a game we want to play all the way to the end. It is worth all the investment that will be necessary—financially and in terms of people's commitment and time.

Construction sites you wouldn't expect...

Important things do not always have to concern only the highest levels, such as strategy. Sometimes they can focus on more specific, smaller organizational "objects." But at the same time, these are widespread throughout the company. Things like meetings, for example. These small construction sites actually turn out to be leverage points for the system because they are places where, with a (relatively) small effort, you can achieve a big result. This is true in general, but it is equally, if not more true, for our construction sites. This is because some of them are overly important, even though they deal with organizational issues that at first glance would seem totally trivial and, precisely because of this, always go unnoticed and unmentioned elsewhere.

Meeting management is one of the most striking examples of the question. We are used to very traditional formats when it comes to meetings. Some people call the meeting, explain why and how they did it, and others just listen. Some people may also speak up. But it never happens that everyone speaks. Or at least, they don't do so freely. And then there are more structured meetings, which also have an agenda or a schedule, and in rare cases some form of supporting documentation. There are also meetings which are infinitely unstructured, with at best a vaguely explanatory title (in the worst cases, I have even seen meetings where the subject was simply "Meeting"), which people attend without ever being clear whether they are about to participate in a meeting to make a decision, report on things, or analyze. In this downward spiral, unfortunately, the end is bitter and predictable. We hold meeting after meeting and continue to waste a lot of time in this way.

Sometimes, everything happens in front of screens where something very often occurs that literally drives me crazy: seeing people who, while they are on camera, turn around at some point and talk to someone else.

Or they turn off the camera, mute the microphone, and float around. They become imaginary presences, in the sense that you don't know what they're doing, what they're feeling, what they're thinking, what they would say and, last but not least, what exactly they're doing there, given that they're removing themselves in every humanly possible way. Yet, despite the obvious futility of their connection, they don't disconnect. Even though it's all too clear to them and the rest of the group that they should be doing anything but being there.

... and construction sites that make all the difference in the world

Every company is full of such imaginary presences; unwelcome guests who, since Covid, are growing in number. We have opened a construction site on this front as well. And we are working on it, diligently. Because teaching meeting management, not just the meeting itself, is a cultural act. It starts before the meeting itself. And it requires giving each individual room to speak, as well as having the ability to listen (not simulated, by consent or, worse, by absence).

Since we started, things have begun to happen. And today, the change is very visible. People talk, show themselves, and do not flee. People no longer talk over each other, but instead raise their hands in Teams and wait for their turn to contribute. Obviously, this also means having people who participate with the explicit aim of facilitating meetings, ensuring they run smoothly and steering the discussion so that it is truly broad and sees active participation. We have therefore developed training specifically aimed at colleagues who tend to be and will be facilitators. Facilitating the meeting to safeguard the process that every meeting must follow.

Now, managing meetings, both in terms of facilitation and participation, may seem like a small thing. In reality, it is not at all: it is something basic but never trivial. But it is also here, above all here, in the basics and in everyday life, that transformation takes place. And this is also where we need to get our hands dirty if we really want to aspire to a new Var Group.

Contributing to the economic and social well-being of the national economy

Aspiring to a new Var Group. And in this new reality—which is now upon us and in which we strongly believe—focusing on innovation, which has always been at the heart of what we do. Because accompanying companies on a path of digital transformation means always keeping an eye on technological innovation, and this will remain so (in the life of a company, purpose is one of the things that never changes) but will increasingly converge, together with everything we achieve in terms of organizational change and people training, into an even more defined goal. Which is precisely why we are doing all this: to contribute to the economic and social well-being of the country in which we work, in this case Italy. Contributing economically, bringing knowledge to digital platforms, because digital platforms are now a prerequisite for competitiveness. And contributing socially, because we train people to be not only better employees within the company, but also better citizens, capable of applying what they learn in our training courses to their everyday lives.

How can we aim so high? How can we do it in practice? The answer is: by bringing innovative solutions to the market, but also to the entire ecosystem, to all the communities we work with every day.

As I write these pages, outside is the scorching heat of late July, summer is in full swing. It is an excellent time to write, taking advantage of the fact that many things slow down a little, and you can find the time and space to focus, especially on the dense, personal and professional issues that I am trying to recount in this book. But what really matters, beyond the pre-holiday rhythm, the need to write, and the weather, is something else: in just a few weeks, on October 3 and 4, we will hold our annual convention in Rimini.

Dreamers

The convention was created with the aim of bringing together people who work in the world of innovation and technology, with the goal of becoming a hub of inspiration and a connection of knowledge. One would therefore expect the organizers (i.e., us) to aim to establish themselves as a source of know-how. And that would be natural. But that's not the case. Because the real goal here is something else entirely. To organize something that makes people dream. That's why we're calling this edition of the convention *Hello Dreamers. The Visionary Side of Digital Evolution.*

And it will be a moment when, personally, I won't care so much if the companies that have chosen Var Group as their partner for their digital evolution come or not. Let's be clear: if they want to, we'll welcome them with open arms. But there is no diktat today, nor will there be a more or less veiled one in the future, like the one that dominates traditional corporate events: you must come, you can't not come, etc. In the last edition, however, the convention was flooded with competitors at one point. But even on that occasion, the reaction was totally opposite to what one would have legitimately expected. Competitors at our convention? Great, the more we talk about it, the better.

A "well-designed" model

Everything is and will be fine. Provided that we achieve our fundamental objective: to make people dream. And here at Var Group, this requires a clear path that passes through an organization that allows and gives everyone, once and for all, the freedom to express themselves. To bring to the surface the creativity that is inherent in being human.

I often hear people say that artificial intelligence will replace human labor. Yes, but only partially. Specifically, it will replace jobs that can be automated in some way. And for that very reason, there is no point in having humans do them. Why use human intelligence to do a job that a machine can do?

At that point, however, it will be up to us to re-skill, and in doing so, to revive human intelligence. Because we are the only beings endowed with empathy, creativity, lateral thinking, and inventiveness. We, not it. Artificial intelligence, however exponential and generative it may be, will probably never be able to do such things. And, in any case, it will never be able to do them as a person would. If what matters is human creativity (in the broadest sense), it is precisely the hallmark of a "well-designed" organizational model to allow people the freedom to express it and to express themselves.

But we are back to square one. Today, without a new organizational model, even with all the platforms in the world, we are going nowhere. Because platforms connect, and this is absolutely true, not only for us in this industry, but for all companies in all sectors. Technology eliminates distance. Technology allows for immediate access to a wealth of information. Technology also allows us to get closer to anyone, to exchange ideas and opinions. Platform technology brings people together, devouring the culture of silos, which divides.

The "silo killer"

Yet even today, the vast majority of companies are still designed and built around silos, divisions that operate in isolation without communicating, often in competition with each other. These organizational structures are light years away from a technology that unites, that seeks interconnection, that demands that people communicate dynamically. These aggregating and multiplying technological potentials, these "silo-killing" platforms, do not develop by approximation. Something else is needed behind the scenes. It requires a precise organizational model, literally tailored to the real context of each company, which guides everything and prevents us from crashing in a clumsy and unconscious attempt to adopt new technologies.

However, it is not just a question of adoption, but also of providing new technologies to the market. Our history itself teaches us that in doing this, in doing all this, it is essential to have an organization that can adapt quickly to market demands, combining various skills to respond effectively and efficiently. This is because today a customer may ask you, for example, to analyze a specific, unique business need. So, you need someone who understands that business. And maybe, at the same time, you need to support them with an artificial intelligence engine. And, again, you need a data scientist who knows how to make their mark.

These two people should immediately work together, understand each other, and come up with an integrated solution for the customer. But they are different people, and they are in different parts of the company. So, if you haven't built an organizational structure based on transparency, clarity of roles, and adaptability, a system that enables these two people to identify market needs and understand each other's skills so that they can generate a meaningful response for the customer, if you haven't done all this, all you are left with is a long and painful process of passing the news of the opportunity up the chain until the boss of the boss of the boss decides what resources and time can be allocated. Hoping, and fervently so, that everything goes smoothly because, if the two figures belong to two completely different structures, speak different languages, and have different codes for understanding each other, in the meantime, time passes, the customer's loses enthusiasm, and ends up moving away and perhaps signing with a competitor.

New generations

Then there are the new generations, which represent a huge challenge. Today, we have at least four different generations working in our company. They range from Boomers to Generation X, Millennials to Zoomers. The first three, to be honest, are very similar, despite their differences, at least in terms of their core values in life. Growing up in the company, in the same company, I mean. Working hard. Being able to afford a home. Getting married, perhaps, or at least starting a family.

I reached the age of twenty-five with the goal of buying a house. At eighteen, I literally couldn't wait to get my driver's license so I could finally have a car and be able to get around on my own. Today, everything has changed. The new generations are totally different. A driver's license is not an essential goal for everyone who comes of age. Nor is a steady job something to strive for right away. The new generations often choose something else. They choose to live, for now, in conditions that allow them to enjoy the present. Bringing together these generations, and above all the diametrically opposed visions they bring with them, is objectively difficult. Even though, unfortunately, demographics show that the younger generations are becoming less and less populous and therefore increasingly finding themselves in a minority position. At the same time, however, they are fundamental, because we cannot do without them and simply because their time has come.

For our part, old organizational models have numbed us, and in the best of cases we wage titanic crusades to try to free ourselves from them. For them, the old models are the devil. Because in their eyes, as it is today, the traditional company is literally disgusting. I look at all this with a deep sense of regret. Because I find myself in the middle of it, and because so many young men and women I talk to, acknowledging all of this, ultimately prefer to turn to self-entrepreneurial experiences. Proof of this is the fact that today there is a proliferation of startups, a phenomenon that has reached incredible proportions and often attracts those who choose any alternative rather than going to work for an established company.

I am convinced that having an entrepreneurial spirit is a great gift (the composition of the Group and of the Var Talks, energized by constructive dialogue between managers and entrepreneurs, speaks clearly in this regard), and that it is an absolute right for everyone to give free rein to this spirit and to actively shape their own future. Unfortunately, I am disappointed every time I see that we, as companies, often let that same entrepreneurial spirit slip away because we are unable to express it within an existing organization that clearly needs an infusion of new blood. The competitiveness of the country's economy cannot be achieved, consolidated, and defended with billions of startups, but rather through the essential task of strengthening the historic companies already present in the territory.

Moreover, if we think about it carefully, this missed opportunity is compounded by another, which is absolutely a mirror-image of the first. The younger generations are also missing out, because a company that is truly focused on the growth of people would offer them a series of opportunities that, on the other hand, individual entrepreneurial initiatives and startups, by their very nature, could take years to incubate, prepare, and create.

In a different way

Nowadays, there is a notable dichotomy between how companies are organized, on the one hand, and how people actually live their everyday "social lives," on the other. If you want a prime example of this, think back to everything we said in the previous chapter, which deals with another dichotomy, that between a culture of permission, on the one hand, and a culture of prohibition, on the other. With social life, the world is pushing towards these two opposites: a culture of permission (you can do anything, absolutely anything, except what is expressly forbidden), and one of corporate organization ("old style", I might add), where a culture of prohibition has always prevailed (you can't do anything unless you are told exactly what to do).

If we want to avoid everything that each of us has had to suffer growing up, the sacred terror of doing and making mistakes, the fear of the cost of failure, the unflinching expectation that things will somehow work themselves out, by "divine providence," if we want to avoid this, it is up to us today to try to understand how to bring permission where prohibition reigns, and create conditions until the former takes over the latter.

Trying to understand means asking questions. Too often we complain that the younger generations are leaving, going abroad. How many people ask themselves why they don't stay in Italy? Just as many pontificate that Generation Z doesn't want to do anything. That's not true at all. They do things. But they do them differently. They often want 100% remote work and find themselves interviewing with companies that don't want to hear about remote work at all. I'm also against 100% remote work, especially for someone who is starting from scratch or has only been working in an organization for a short time, but more generally in any company. I am also opposed to the total absence of smart working, which is an absolute deprivation in relation to the globally shared need to balance work and private life.

Moreover, if you work in a truly open organization, with clear and transparent rules as well as precise and shared objectives, all co-created by you and those who work with you, then you really have the opportunity to organize yourself as you see fit. Obviously, taking into account the fact that, from experience, the company is something that must be lived and breathed, and this can only be achieved by spending time there.

The new generations are a huge issue, bringing with them a need to rethink the company that cannot be ignored.

Changes

Youth malaise, on closer inspection and especially in a period such as this one, does not fall on deaf ears. People of all ages are unhappy in the workplace today. Well-founded (and well-known) research by Gallup shows that, according to the data, there is a great deal of dissatisfaction within workplaces and companies. This phenomenon is exacerbated in the younger generations and is unleashed to the nth degree. And it is completely understandable, because the way we live has changed. Despite all this, we persist in thinking in terms of models from the 1950s, if not the early 20th century or even the first industrial revolution.

Things have changed, and the exaggerated scope of this change is due precisely to IT, the field in which we work at Var Group, which has definitively "changed change," so to speak, transforming a logic—the linear one that had characterized something like two hundred thousand years of human history—into an exponential one. The order has changed, and as a result, the issues we face have changed. These too are strictly exponential.

The disengagement photographed by Gallup is an indication that too much responsibility is being placed on too few people and too little on all the others. In other words, we continue to filter the world hierarchically, betting on a sort of power that is poorly allocated and therefore too often does not go where it is needed. The result is that we lose focus on the real problems. And often all we do is chase after deviations. But the problems of companies are problems of the system: even if we wanted to, and even if we forced ourselves to, they cannot be blamed on exceptions.

Two things will happen

In 2024, from the stage of the Maggio Fiorentino, we launched a snapshot of the future that caused quite a stir. When the new organizational model is fully implemented, we will realize this because two things will happen. First, everyone will be fully capable of managing their own vacation time. People who are part of a team will decide when to take vacation, without having to get approval first. They will do this because they will have taken on enough responsibility and will have enough data at their disposal to be able to make the decision independently, evaluating the best option for themselves and for the company. Maybe at first they will make mistakes and will have to work while on vacation. But this will mean that next time they will think a little longer and plan a little better; on their own responsibility, though, not someone else's (this, in fact, is already happening at our company).

The second: self-determination of salary. In a truly open organization, people will be able to determine their own salaries. This means making all salaries across the entire company completely transparent. The very concept of self-determination of salary caused quite a stir among the Kick Off audience. There was murmuring, confusion, and commotion. Here too, we started testing this on a few teams, clearly indicating the self-determined salary ranges. They consulted them, studied them, and reacted with amazement, because they realized that when you ask for a raise, you automatically think about what the difference is between yourself and others, while in practice, the reality is somewhat different and more complicated.

A change of pace, and of paradigm

Open organization calls for distributed leadership. In other words, you decide independently, but within simple and clear rules. There was a time when companies operated based on a concept that closely resembled the logic of a traffic light. Red light, stop; green light, go. Go, or stay put. It was a top-down logic, coordinated from above. It was based on hierarchy, with individuals serving as tools in the hands of the organization to generate output. The new model, which is a paradigm shift, works differently. It requires at least a couple of inversions.

It is the organization that becomes a tool in the hands of the individual, and for generating impact. Of course, there must be output. But we measure ourselves and orient ourselves towards something else. Towards the outcome, the result. The goal is no longer the ice cream itself, for example, but the smile of the person eating it. We work on responsibility, which, unlike a traditional task, is a "self-commitment," and that no one can "commit for another" (these are the words of Bill Gore, founder of the company that invented Gore-Tex). The "old" companies are still all optimized for tasks; open organizations, the "place" where we want Var Group to land as soon as possible, are optimized for responsibility.

To achieve all this, to create improvement directly in the hands of those who work, we need to act with motivation. There is a lot of talk about motivation today; but many organizations and companies still seem to have failed to grasp the full meaning of the concept. The motivation we need is lasting, intrinsic, and capable of taking root in people. Not rewards or punishments, to be clear. And intrinsic motivation (as Daniel Pink reminds us in his book *Drive*) requires autonomy, competence (mastery of the field), and purpose. At Var Group, and here we return to the rules of the road, so to say, we are doing a lot of work on autonomy. However, as you know by now, this is based on an oxymoron because, in order to work properly, autonomy needs boundaries.

Traffic lights, roundabouts, catalysts

Freedom needs boundaries to channel it and allow it to express itself. This is where we return to the metaphor of the traffic light and everything it represents, which is a thing of the past. Our new model works like a roundabout: through voluntary coordination. The roundabout ensures that you take responsibility, but within clear rules. In driving school, they teach you how to behave at a roundabout, looking right and checking that there are no vehicles, with the simple and clear rule of giving way to those coming from the right. Stop. No one tells you to go or stay put. You look, check, and act accordingly.

A roundabout is created when three conditions are met.

The first: transparency. Roundabouts require people to see the flow of traffic and understand what is happening. Roundabouts exist when there are no obstacles to visibility.

The second: clarity. Knowing the rules of the game, which must be strictly known to everyone, i.e., mutual expectations, how roundabouts work, why there are few rules, right of way, etc.

The third (which takes us out of the metaphor): adaptability. That is the ability to adaptively change the rules of the game as you go along, continuously, as if it were a maintenance exercise (which, in fact, it is).

We are moving towards the best possible roundabout. By encouraging people to take responsibility for themselves and leading the organization towards distributed leadership and empowerment. As mentioned, this must be done within a framework of clear rules, but that have at least been co-created and co-written. This is also where the novelty lies: there is no one who writes the rules for everyone. If we can establish these few but clear rules, and apply them successfully, then we will continuously evolve. Going straight to the heart of innovation, as a goal, and to the creation of value for the country's economic system, for the communities that make it up, and for individuals, as a new purpose. This is how my dream becomes reality: to leave room for people to make things happen, precisely because there was first the ability to leave room for their growth.

Facilitating is an act of growth and empowerment. Facilitating means allowing autonomy. It means helping people exercise that autonomy, to think concretely about what to do with their freedom. And it is not a single, unidirectional act. It is a two-way exercise, in which one speaks and listens, and one helps and receives. One helps and receives. It is an important, fundamental exchange, on which the boundaries of the future are drawn. And it is a process that works not on a single catalyst, but on many. It cannot and must not be from me to the entire population of Var Group, but from people to people, with the help of those who facilitate and those who play the role of ambassador throughout the entire organization.

One leader, a thousand leaders

This is a momentous transition: from one leader to a thousand leaders. Let me explain: in my view, someone "ruling over many" is not a leader but a boss. The transition is from one boss to many leaders.

I previously told you about my dream, the one where I walk around the company feeling calm and people spontaneously stop me to tell me about the excellent progress of projects I know little or nothing about. In reality, my hope is slightly different, and a little more transgressive, if you will. Because when we really function, when we are an organization open to distributed leadership, people won't come to tell me anything. Because there will be no reason to come to me. There will be no need at all. Today, many people stop me. Some because they still need support or advice. Or because they want to show me that one path or another we are taking is beginning to bear fruit.

This is the present. In the future, "tomorrow," the opposite will be totally natural. They won't come and tell me things. They won't stop me in the hallways. They won't follow me to the cafeteria, and they won't peek into the room where our "round table" is. Because things evolving on their own will be the absolute, complete norm. Because we'll have OKRs that tell us point by point what will happen over the next four months.

We have set ourselves a goal. An ambitious one, as always. To end up in the economics textbooks with our model within five years. As I write, one year has already passed. As I write, there are four left, but I have a

feeling we can make it even sooner. Even though there is a lot to do, because in the meantime the company is growing and there is a lot to work
on. In the coming years, we will build and spread distributed leadership,
where every individual is a leader in their own role. Where every leader
will have a firm grip on activities and projects and will be able to respon-
sibly manage their evolution. If all this works, truly and completely, absurdly but correctly, there will no longer be any need for me as I am today.

The "management apocalypse"

There will no longer be a need for me and all management as it is today.
We will have to change, transform ourselves. Because, at least as far as
I am concerned, what I do today—facilitating, strategizing, planning—
will be greatly diminished tomorrow. I will certainly be the only one
who, by virtue of my position, will have to define Var Group's strategy.
And I believe that tomorrow I will do it exactly as I do today: talking
to people, understanding things, listening to the market, etc. But if the
model works, that's all I'll have left. To take it to the extreme: in a model
that works perfectly, the organization will not be in my hands, but in the
hands of everyone. If the model works, if it really works as it should, the
middle management layers as we know them will disappear, perhaps to
be converted into something else.

Imagine human activity after the arrival of artificial intelligence. Human intelligence is wasted on tasks that a machine can perform on its
own. So it moves upstream, to prompting, which is needed to build the
intelligence that allows the machine to work effectively and avoid the
problem of "garbage in, garbage out," where poor stimuli generate dis-
appointing results; and it moves downstream, to refining the machine's
output, with that human touch that machines will never be able to replicate. Those who are "leaders" will become something different. Because
being a leader, as it is understood today, means command and control. Indeed, it means *being* command and control. Command. Control. That's
why there is social anxiety about going to the leader and reporting what
has been done.

We will have OKRs, we have already started writing them, to be cas-
caded down to all levels. OKRs based on which the entire population
will decide what to do in their daily work, level by level, BU by BU, team

by team. This will continue down to the individual level, where each person will clearly know what direction to take in the four-month period and will be able to decide how to do so. Everyone will also know, through written rules that are transparent, visible, and accessible at all times, how to interact with others, how to manage any conflicts, and so on. In light of this, management—as we usually imagine it in a somewhat negative sense—will no longer serve any purpose.

For all this to happen, however, there will need to be a simultaneous explosion of a completely opposite phenomenon. An explosion of managerialism, if you will. The end of management equals distributed managerialism, i.e., a tremendous ability to focus on one's goals, at any level, and to manage oneself. No more managers, distributed managerial skills.

The right alliance

There is still a lot of work to be done. Above all because the global scale of this change, of all this change, in a clear and complete way, is perhaps still known to only a few, very few.

Maybe just me. In all this, I consider myself extremely lucky because I have managed to find an ally who understands what is going through my mind. Who agrees with its significance. Who provides us with the tools we need to turn it into reality. And who supports us in making it happen. There are a few of us who understand this clearly. A few of us, plus Kopernicana, the ally I was referring to. That's why I often talk to them, because it's difficult to explain it fully to many other people who may still be addicted to the corporate life of the past.

It's amazing to think that the alliance with Kopernicana started just a year ago. When I met Francesco Frugiuele, the founder, I didn't know who he was, and he didn't know who I was either. As a result, he didn't even know what I had in mind. I simply told him everything. He replied that the chances of failure were higher than those of success. That doing it across the entire Var Group was impossible, and it would be wiser to limit ourselves to a well-defined space. For an hour straight, he tried to dissuade me in every way possible. Because starting would have meant living perpetually on the edge of a precipice.

I listened to everything, from the first word to the last. Then I replied. He didn't know me, so I understood that perhaps all his caution and warnings stemmed from thinking that I was a little presumptuous and had little real knowledge of the vast area in which I wanted to prove myself at all costs. I reiterated that Var Group was already way ahead of traditional, "rigid" companies. That we had, if nothing else, at least one thing: awareness of what we wanted to do, of what was needed to evolve. And I deliberately used "we" because I had that awareness, but I wasn't the only one. What we needed, rather, was someone to help us.

"You can do it"

Then, one fine day, after some time had passed, he came up to me and said only: "You were right, your company can do it." He didn't know me, and he had never come to a Kick Off. I invited him and Priel to the 2023 event. They were amazed. Amazed by the "fun," of course. But also because, until then, Francesco had only seen me as the CEO of a company that, in 2023, had a turnover of 720 million euros. Period. At the Kick Off, he saw Francesca walking among the crowd, asking one person how their dog was, another how their grandfather was, and yet another how things were going. I was still Francesca, and that was the old lesson I had learned from a phenomenal cousin during a summer spent at markets around Tuscany. But Francesco hadn't seen that yet, so he couldn't know.

Now he saw someone who knew everyone's business, because she talked to everyone, and everyone felt perfectly comfortable telling her about it. He saw all this and wondered insistently how it was possible. He saw her moving totally naturally among people who had no problem stopping her and talking to her, just as they had no problem telling her to get lost, and he kept asking himself questions. It was there, I think, that he realized that we have a slightly different chemistry. And that chemistry was the exact reason why we could probably do it. Because there was no distance between me and my colleagues. I didn't want to be addressed formally, I had no intention of showing off, and I continued to consider myself always and only one person among many.

All this has never changed, as far as I'm concerned. In the Var Talks, I am nothing more than a Var Talker. I am not and do not intend to be the one who raises her hand and says: "Oh, I'm in charge here." I'm not like that, and I would never allow myself to be. It would make me feel disgusted. I listen, I'm "good," and I keep quiet. Maybe not exactly "good," but what matters is that I am neither more nor less than the others. This transition is still difficult for some people to accept today.

The question I ask myself lately is always the same: "How can I help you?" It's basically the question a good facilitator asks. Or, at the very least: "Why are you telling me this?" Which is still a variation on the "original" question, but also opens up the possibility of "Have you tried asking the right person?" I ask, and if necessary, I return them to the sender.

Seeking a visionary mind

Not long ago, while we were working on *Hello Dreamers*, the October 2024 convention, the need arose to find a visionary mind, a figure who could legitimately take part in the event with an inspirational speech. I wrote to Giovanni, asking him if, from his vantage point he could think of any names to suggest for us to approach. In the end, we ran a multiple search on the main artificial intelligence engines. One of them responded with a list of names and detailed reasons for each one. It added that, considering his career, experience, passions, and knowledge of the field, a valid option could be Giovanni himself!

Giovanni had glanced at the prompt's result and, after taking a screenshot, sent it to me. He had no intention of pleading his case, but rather wanted to share the other names, which in any case formed a critical mass to be analyzed, explored, and filtered. When I received the screenshot, I read everything once, froze, and then reread it all from the beginning. Several times. That suggestion, thrown out there by chance and just as casually ignored by Giovanni, was brilliant to me. An epiphany. I talked to Giovanni, but he was reluctant. Too much the chairman. I turned the question back on him: "Come as a visionary, not a chairman." He thought about it. For a month. Then he accepted the challenge.

The day arrived when we had also scheduled a meeting with Sara and Alessandro (Communication & PR Manager and Head of Sales & Marketing, respectively) to tell Giovanni in detail what was planned for the event, so as to provide him with all the necessary information to prepare his speech, also taking advantage of the fact that, shortly thereafter, he would be going on vacation and would therefore have the time and opportunity to start thinking about it.

In a meeting like that, with the roles reversed, I would keep quiet, with my ideas in my head but quiet, listening to everything the others had to say (which would be useful for me to make my contribution in the best way possible). Then I would say my piece and find a solution together with the others. Instead, when the moment came, Giovanni didn't even let us sit down. "So, I'll start by telling you what I think..." And blah, blah, blah, blah, blah. For half an hour of rapid-fire commentary. I had to leave early, I would let Sara and Alessandro finish, but I wanted to be there at the beginning. After those thirty minutes of monologue, just before leaving, I couldn't help but say to him: "Excuse me, Giovanni, but if you listen to the logical flow of the event and the plenary session, you might be able to articulate your ideas better..."

Voilà la différence

That's the difference. Giovanni is a force of nature, the perfect visionary, in general but especially for *Hello Dreamers*. I was convinced that he would rock that stage, no ifs, ands, or buts about it. The problem lies elsewhere. It's in the approach. Giovanni is undoubtedly the champion of the "old" Var Group. It was a company that had a different management style—in the broadest sense and in terms of organization more specifically—that was in line with the times.

Giovanni has his rough edges, like everyone else. And if you read carefully the thoughts he shared with the audience at the Maggio Fiorentino, you will also know that he has been able to see and recognize many of these "rough edges" for what they are. Because Giovanni is also a great supporter of our new path. He cannot be anything else, because he recognizes principles that he knows and respects, and values and methodologies in which he has always believed; even when he was unable or did not know how to apply them—and these are his words, because we have talked about it a million times. The last time, when I asked him point-blank why he was behaving in a certain way, he looked me in the eyes for a moment, then gave me his best answer. It went like this:

"Francesca, you're right, my way of relating to people is 'chairman-centric'. But I was trained and grew up in a different era. With different technologies. Over the years, the principles haven't changed; the ones that are taking Var Group into the future are, after all, the same as those of the past. Three things make the big difference. Today's technologies and their impact on society, people, and communications and interactions."

According to Giovanni, organizational and behavioral models that work, the "winning" ones, must understand and embrace these changes, which are opportunities. "Do you remember Computer Var, the 'mother' of Var Group? It was born at the same time as email and the first websites, and was managed with faxes and physical files... Var Group evolved from there, taking its very first shape alongside things like e-commerce and collaboration. Those were times when technology and culture made it difficult to build a model with high and continuous interactivity, with distributed leadership, if you like. Because our effective and competitive reality needed a different model, more like a solar system, at the most a network. I shaped and developed my operational skills during those moments. I can adapt, but I can make my real contribution with a new relationship, different from the everyday."

That sort of stream of consciousness took me by surprise. I continued to listen to Giovanni as he told me that he has always cultivated a personal purpose: to try to understand new technologies and their impact on the lives of people and organizations. To assist this process, and to make his expertise available. Then he stopped, looked me straight in the eye, and asked me point-blank: "Do you know to whom? To the new Var Group. Do you know why? Because it's my way, and the best method I have available to contribute to the evolution of the group. I believe that, since the beginning of time, successful organizations are those that have been able to understand and make the best use of existing technologies. And so, I believe that we at Var Group know how to do this really well, we are doing it, and we will definitely continue to do so."

Giovanni has his rough edges, like everyone else. But for all this, and much more, he is part of the new path. A path that is "the" Challenge of the Var Group today. With a capital C, as it is a challenge for everyone. With all the quotation marks necessary, because behind it there are countless other challenges. For us, that other path is not only possible, but it is the future itself. And we are running towards it, with courage but also with discipline, in part creativity and in part audacity. And with the same fervor as that woman who bounded up the steps of a heart hospital a distant April 7 many years ago, in search of the ultimate truth.

Welcome to Braveship

When I started telling this story, not to myself and in my head, but to you, the readers, I wasn't sure where all the references, flashbacks, and connections I've shared with you so far would end up. This is also because, in reality, the story you've read isn't over yet. It can't be, because it has a lot to do with my personal story, and there is, there has been, and there will continue to be, a lot to write about that. Nor can it afford to be over, given the story of Var Group, which as you have seen with your own eyes, still has a long way to go to achieve its goals, which are as ambitious as we are, and as a result, translate into long and complex dynamics.

Perhaps what we expect when we pick up a book is to find a complete story, with a beginning and an end. If this is true, and custom suggests that it is, then what you hold in your hands is not a book in the strict sense of the word. I like to think of it as a multiverse, like the ones you see in Marvel movies, where there are photographs of different worlds, sometimes parallel, sometimes coinciding, with a single underlying law: things happen in one part and have effects on other parts. Worlds that are formally different coexist: organizational trends with business stories, my personal experience with my entrepreneurial experience. And then business and fairness cases, "agile lessons" and failures, successes and scars, with related lessons to follow.

What I find most interesting, perhaps, is that this varied combination of things that we usually place in different compartments is, in my humble opinion, the most faithful representation of reality. Reality is a place where everything happens simultaneously, where we "happen" simultaneously, in the plurality of things that we are, every single day. If this is correct, if this is not a book but a celebration of the journey that will lead us to become an open organization, a model of innovation, the fruit of the many efforts made to enable and facilitate it, then while we await the future developments that will be needed to tell you the rest of the story, it is worth planting a flag now.

That flag has only one thing written on it. But, in my opinion, it sums up all these galaxies, these multiverses in themselves. Something that starts with us, but is also Var Group's gift to the world, faithful to its new purpose of contributing to the economic and social well-being of the country, bringing innovative solutions to the market, society, and the ecosystem. You know perfectly well by now that we celebrate courage but also discipline, and we exalt creativity as much as audacity. Well, the exact point of intersection of all this, which is so much and which guides the very way we look at ourselves and the world, that point exists and has a name.

Incidentally, this is the point at which the open company we are pursuing, and the practical principle of distributed leadership that characterizes it, take a turn that is perfectly and harmoniously in line with Var Group. The point we want to include in textbooks is called, for us and from now on for the rest of the population: *Braveship*. To those of you who have read this far and now know a little about me, about us, and about the Group, I can only say: welcome to Var Group, *welcome to Braveship*.

January 2025

In China, January 29, 2025 marked the beginning of the Year of the Snake, also known there as the "little dragon." Legend has it that those born during this period are the wisest and most fascinating of all. They love to communicate, have a marked preference for anything new and interesting, a talent for seeing things from different points of view, and incredible persistence in pursuing their goals, which are always concrete (the snake does not waste time or engage in flights of fancy). We are not experts in Chinese horoscopes, incidentally, but in January 2025, with the Year of the Snake having just begun (unbeknownst to us), in order to give shape to everything I have told you so far, we launched the *Var Group Organizational Constitution* through Var Talks, which establishes some rules, that are few but well defined and clear to all, as I have told you in the previous pages.

This *Constitution* lands in a place where every individual finds room to express their potential, and where everyone's contribution becomes a spark that ignites innovation and shared growth. Like a manifesto celebrating the strength of people and their roles, bringing together skills, aspirations, and visions in a harmonious symphony. Formally, it is a constitution; in reality, it is our compass towards an organization that transcends traditional hierarchical structures, offering each person the opportunity to shine and feel part of something bigger, without losing their uniqueness.

For each of us, it is an invitation to build together, with awareness and freedom, a working model that values the individual in their role, recognizing their rights and responsibilities, and creates fertile ground for authentic and inspired collaboration. It is neither a rigid manual nor an immutable policy. Rather, in keeping with our style, it is a flexible framework designed to adapt to the needs and challenges we will encounter. We wrote it with ourselves in mind, but also drawing inspiration from the experiences of other organizations that have adopted self-management and distributed leadership practices, adapting external ideas to our context through cross-functional co-creation, thanks to people from different areas of Var Group.

As the "guardian of legal power," I ratified it, making it the tangible symbol of a collective agreement to define (and redefine!) our organizational path. I did so knowing, as everyone does, that over time it may be modified, amended and transformed, always with the aim of keeping its spirit alive. That of an open, agile organization, imbued with humanity. Our *Constitution* represents the foundation of our organizational system, designed as an open and collaborative platform. Thanks to it, we define the conceptual principles, operating rules, and constraints that guide our organization toward an agile, inclusive, and constantly evolving model. With the aim of promoting innovation that is ours, and as such arises spontaneously from collaboration and self-organization.

The document has been carefully crafted and deserves to be explained in more detail, starting with the stages of its adoption. You can't just drop a bomb like this on four thousand people and leave it at that. We need to proceed step by step, across the various business units and shared service platforms, to help people understand it and start adopting it. We need to proceed step by step, and this is part of our plan for 2025.

It is not just another construction site, but "the" construction site. The one that will bring to fruition everything we have thought, structured, and developed over the last two years. Something like this deserves to be explained properly, but this is a topic we will return to shortly, in other pages than those of this book, which is now practically complete. Innovation is also connection; and so the invitation I extend to you, if you are curious to learn more, can only be: stay connected...

Some readings (almost a bibliography)

P. Coelho, *Monte Cinque*, Milan, La Nave di Teseo, 2018.

A. Cravera, *Essere leader in un mondo complesso. Scegliere la direzione per persone e organizzazioni*, Milan, Egea, 2024.

S. Friedman, *Total leadership. Raggiungere risultati e soddisfa- zione sul lavoro, in famiglia, nei rapporti sociali e per sé stessi*, Milan, Egea, 2023.

A. Gangemi, *Organizzazioni aperte. Il lavoro progettato da chi lavora*, Milan, Ayros, 2023.

R. Hastings, E. Meyer, *L'unica regola è che non ci sono regole. Netflix e la cultura della reinvenzione*, Milan, Garzanti, 2020.

R. Kipling, *Se*, Turin, Einaudi, 2017.

P. Luthra, *Diversifying Diversity: Your Guide to Being an Active Ally of Inclusion in the Workplace*, self-published, 2021.

P. Luthra, *The Art of Active Allyship: 7 Behaviours to Empower You to Push The Pendulum Towards Inclusion At Work*, self-published, 2022.

P. Luthra, S.L. Muhr, *Leading Through Bias. 5 Essential Skills to Block Bias and Improve Inclusion at Work*, Cham, Palgrave Macmillan, 2024.

D. Marquet, *The leadership. La vera storia di un capitano capace di distribuire l'autorità al suo equipaggio*, Milan, Ayros, 2022.

J. Minnaar, P. de Morree, *Corporate Rebels: Make work more fun*, Corporate Rebels Nederland B.V., 2020.

D.H. Pink, *Drive. Cosa davvero guida la nostra motivazione*, Milan, Ayros, 2022.

Control room

We are in the century of artificial intelligence, but above all (and as far as we are concerned) in that of collective intelligence. Too much is said about the former, too little about the latter. And that's a great shame, because this book was born precisely from a collective intelligence in which:

Francesca Moriani contributed her head, heart, and "gut";

Simone Petrelli painted and colored the canvas;

Alessandro Gencarelli and Joshua Volpara, who laid the foundations for the project during a lunch in full creative delirium, pulled out their best director's chairs, just like on any self-respecting set, and orchestrated the alchemy.

Many minds behind a single book. Because, as we have learned in these pages, *power lies in the hands of all people.*

Author's apologies

A normal book, at this exact point, would contain the classic acknowledgments. However, this is not a normal book. As a consequence, I intend to use this space to... publicly apologize to those who, for some reason (space constraints, memory lapses, etc.), do not appear in these pages. These are people who, in fact and absolutely on par with those who are mentioned in some way, have contributed to the genesis of the story told here, travelling a part of the road (and of life) together with me. They therefore deserve, first of all, my sincere apologies, and secondly, my heartfelt gratitude.

Thanks to them, and thank you from the bottom of my heart!

F.M.

www.ingramcontent.com/pod-product-compliance
Lightning Source LLC
Chambersburg PA
CBHW031851200326
41597CB00012B/361